# Reading Through Colossians and Ephesians

*By the same author*

Reading Through Galatians
Reading Through Hebrews

# Reading Through Colossians and Ephesians

C. R. Hume

SCM PRESS LTD

0 334 02720 9

First published 1998 by
SCM Press Ltd
9–17 St Albans Place London N1 0NX

Typeset at the Spartan Press Ltd,
Lymington, Hants
Printed in Great Britain by
Biddles Ltd, Guildford and King's Lynn

# Contents

# Foreword

The principles I have followed in writing this guide have already been outlined in the forewords to my previous books, *Reading Through Hebrews* and *Reading Through Galatians*. I have attempted to keep my translation as literal as possible, so that the Greek terms of the original can be easily related to the English version, and I have tried to answer the question, 'What would this mean to the first-century reader?' The question, 'How does the message of these letters relate to our contemporary concerns or problems?', I leave to others. It is my belief that we can only attempt to answer the latter when we have properly dealt with the former question.

The guide is intended for use by an individual or a group of students, anyone who is prepared to take the study of the scriptures seriously. Lest, however, I deter the faint-hearted, I hasten to add that I have tried to avoid the more academic issues which are the province of specialists in the study of the New Testament, and at the same time to show the depth of meaning and insight in two of the most fascinating letters of the early church.

# Introduction

## When were these letters written?

We can be certain that they are not early works. The references to the author's imprisonment and the statements in these letters that their author was Paul, together point to a period in the mid-sixties of the first century. Several commentators have put forward strong arguments for believing that Paul wrote these letters while he was in prison in Rome awaiting trial and date them to around 63. If either, or both, of these works is a forgery, as some commentators have claimed, the date can be later than this. This leads on to the next question:

## Did Paul write these letters?

The whole issue has been discussed so earnestly over the last 150 years and the waters of debate are so muddied that it might help if we cleared our minds of preconceptions and adopted a fresh and radical approach to the question. Let us start by asking, 'What do we actually know?'

1. The early commentators were unanimous about the identity of the author; they agreed that Paul wrote these letters.

2. Those who doubt the authorship disagree amongst themselves as to whether both letters or just one of them should be regarded as non-Pauline.

3. It is claimed that there are important differences in thought, style, content and vocabulary in Colossians and Ephesians when we compare them with other letters which have generally been accepted as written by Paul.

4. There is a serious doubt whether the recipients of the letter entitled Ephesians actually were the Christians living in Ephesus. This doubt was also shared by some early Christian scholars. There were at least two letters circulating in the valley of the river Lycus, the area in which were situated the towns of Colossae, Hierapolis and Laodicaea, if we accept the authenticity of the information given in Col. 4.16. One of these letters was Colossians and the other a letter which had been sent to the church in Laodicaea. This could be the letter we now know as Ephesians.

5. Both letters purport to have been written by Paul – they contain statements which make such a claim. In other words, they are either forgeries or genuine. They are not simply letters which happen to be anonymous, like the letter to the Hebrews. There is an intermediate view – they could be genuine letters which contain material introduced by another hand.

6. If they were not written by Paul, what could be the motive for composing these letters and attributing them to him? It was certainly not unknown in the ancient world for imitators of famous writers to produce works written in the style of their models or, for example, to continue a history left unfinished by the original writer. Were these written by someone using Paul's name to gain acceptability for some heretical or unorthodox doctrine? But our letters contain no such material. Various ingenious reasons have been suggested why the letters, particularly Ephesians, could have been written by someone claiming to be Paul, but they are purely speculative. For instance, it has been claimed that they were written to supply doctrinal material which the author felt Paul

himself would have supplied if he had lived long enough. Others claim that they incorporate new doctrines and were attributed to Paul in order to give them the seal of approval. Even if it can be shown that they contain new doctrinal matter, there is still no evidence that Paul did not write them. This lack of evidence also leaves unsupported another suggestion, namely, that a friend of Paul wrote them in his style because Paul was too busy to write them himself or too far away. It would take up more space than is appropriate for a book in this series to discuss in more detail the fascinating question of authorship. Other commentaries deal with this subject at greater length.

**7.** We cannot prove the authorship of *any* ancient document to the satisfaction of the determined sceptic, who, when faced with a passage clearly resembling other works generally accepted as those of the author under consideration, claims that it must be an imitation, and when a passage is dissimilar, argues that the dissimilarity proves that someone else must have written it. This is a 'heads, I win; tails, you lose' argument.

Leaving aside the question whether the recipients were the Ephesians, a question we can deal with when we turn our attention to the relevant statement in the first chapter of that letter, the question of authenticity mostly hinges on the third statement in the above list, i.e. that these letters differ from the letters generally accepted as written by Paul. If there are differences, are they so great that we must accept that Paul could not have written them? Without going into too much detail in this introduction we can state that they fall into the following categories:

## 1. *Differences in vocabulary*
Firstly, there are words used in these letters that are used nowhere else. Such words, incidentally, are called **hapax legomena**, '[words] spoken once'. There are words found in

Colossians that are not found in Ephesians, and *vice versa*. There are also words found only in Colossians and Ephesians. On the other hand, there are also words found in Galatians and Romans that are not found in other letters, yet we do not regard that as evidence for saying that Paul could not have written those letters. There are reckoned to be 42 **hapax legomena** in Ephesians and 48 in Colossians, but this is not disproportional when we remember that there are around 100 in Romans, 108 in I Corinthians, 95 in II Corinthians and 33 in Galatians. Incidentally, since Colossians is a much shorter letter than Ephesians, the proportion of **hapax legomena** in Colossians is higher than the raw total might indicate. This large number of **hapax legomena**, more than half of which are in Chapter 2, may be due to the fact that the novel subject-matter of Colossians demands a new and specialized vocabulary. Secondly, it is claimed that there are words used in in our letters, or phrases made up of such words, which have a different meaning from the one they carry in other Pauline letters. This is rather a subjective matter since the meaning of a word is frequently a matter for argument. We shall look at such cases as they occur in the course of our enquiry. Finally, if Paul was living in Rome at the time these letters were written, one would expect him to have picked up new expressions. The Greek spoken in one part of the Roman empire could differ considerably from the Greek spoken in another part, in the same way that English differs both in vocabulary and syntax throughout the world today. As a result Paul could have unconsciously picked up words and expressions which were used by Greek speakers in Rome. Anyone from the UK who has lived in the United States (or *vice versa*) for a year will have experienced this almost unconscious process of assimilation.

## 2. *Differences in style and tone*

Although this is the most contentious area of enquiry and one where consensus is most difficult, it is possible to assess these differences. Broadly speaking, those who regard Ephesians as inferior in style (or content, for that matter) to other Pauline letters are the ones who question its authenticity. For example, De Wette, one of the sceptics of the last century, thought that it was 'verbose amplification', *wortreiche Erweiterung*, of the letter to the Colossians. 'Amplification' is justified; 'verbose' is debatable. Matters touched on in Colossians are often explained in more detail in Ephesians. Incidentally, F. C. Synge, a more recent commentator, takes the opposite view and claims that Colossians was written by an imitator of Ephesians. Native Greek speakers, on the other hand, such as were the majority of early commentators, would be the first to sense the sort of difference in style which is due to the fact that a work is an imitation, and they did not doubt the authenticity of either of our two letters.

We should give some credit to the sensibilities of contemporaries or near contemporaries, and it is appropriate to quote C. S. Lewis[1] comparing modern reviewers, who were frequently wrong in their assumptions about the genesis of his own works, with modern biblical commentators. 'Consider with what overwhelming advantages the mere reviewers start. They reconstruct the history of a book written by someone whose mother-tongue is the same as theirs; a contemporary, educated like themselves, living in something like the same mental and spiritual climate. They have everything to help them. The superiority in judgment and diligence which you are going to attribute to the Biblical critics will have to be almost superhuman if it is to offset the fact that they are everywhere faced with customs, language, race-characteristics, class-characteristics, a religious background, habits of composition, and basic assumptions, which no scholarship will ever enable any man now alive to know as surely and intimately and instinctively as the reviewer can know mine.' This is why we should not dismiss lightly the views of scholars

---

[1] *Christian Reflections*, Geoffrey Bles 1967, p. 161.

who lived during the early part of the Christian era and whose native language was Greek.

Chrysostom, whose literary skills were remarkable by any standard, had no difficulty in accepting Paul as the author of Ephesians, while acknowledging the work's individual character: 'the letter is loaded with the most sublime thoughts; for what he has uttered nowhere else, here he makes clear'. Erasmus, who wrote, of course, over a thousand years later than Chrysostom, also makes a similar point: 'certainly the style is so different from the other letters of Paul that it could be thought to belong to someone else, if it were not for the fact that the psychology and individual character of Paul's mind (*pectus atque indoles Paulinae mentis*) assert absolutely that it is his'.

### 3. *Differences in content*

These are basically to be defined as doctrinal or philosophical discrepancies. But are they simply the normal differences you would expect to find in the later works of any writer which would have developed over a period of time, or are they so radically different that the same person could not have expressed them? In concentrating on the differences between our two letters (and Philippians, for that matter) and the rest of the Pauline canon, most critics seem not to have noticed the striking resemblance between these letters and the type of literature produced by writers whose vision of the world and of God has been moulded by the experience of prison. Martin, however, is one who has noticed this connection, comparing, in his commentary on Colossians (p. 159), the writing of Dietrich Bonhoeffer during his Tegel imprisonment with Paul's own 'prison christology'. I believe we can go further in exploring and comparing the distinctive characteristics of writing by those who have suffered from a period of imprisonment. From Bunyan to modern Russian dissidents, from victims of Nazi persecution to hostages of terrorists, we can find many examples of authors whose painful and intense emotions, frequently conveying strong religious beliefs with a sense of urgency, or whose efforts to construct a theoretical world of security and certainty to live in, remind one of Colossians and Ephesians in their style, tone and content. Could it be that this is the basic reason why we feel that these letters are so different? We could spend a great deal of time discussing the matter in general terms, but the issue is best dealt with as we go through the letters. For the sake of convenience in reference, if for no other reason, I shall address the author of both letters as Paul. Those who wish to pursue the question of authorship further are referred to the commentaries mentioned in the bibliography at the end of this book.

## The central themes of the letters

F. W. Farrar[2] neatly sums up the themes of the two letters: 'The dominant thought of the Colossians is Christ over all; that of the Ephesians, the Universal Church in Christ.' At the risk of over-simplifying we might take that as a reasonable place to start.

## 1. Colossians

Because Colossians is a short letter, the main theme soon emerges: the unique position of Christ not only as head of the church but as the one by whom all things were created. As with Ephesians, there is a strong sense of intense emotion carrying the argument along. Paul's prose frequently seems to take off into poetry; so much so, that some commentators have concluded that he is actually quoting at one point from a hymn. At the same time, the style of Colossians is more terse and abbreviated than that of the letter to the Ephesians. If we examine closely those passages which have parallels in the

---

[2]*The Life and Work of St Paul*, Cassell & Company, 1884, p. 589.

other letter, we notice that Ephesians often gives more detail. This can be seen, for example, when we compare the way the body metaphor is handled in Col. 2.19 and Eph. 4.16.

In the first chapter Christ's superiority is defined, and then in the second chapter Paul returns to his theme and underlines the completeness of his work of redemption. He warns the Colossians against the performance of rituals based on the old notion that one could win God's approval in this way. The rest of the letter concerns itself with pastoral concerns and a call to keep the faith.

This summary of the theme of the letter may give the impression that Colossians is an easy letter to understand. Because it often touches only briefly upon points which are more fully developed in Ephesians, we might assume that all is crystal clear. Nothing could be further from the truth. Most of the difficulties in this letter centre on two areas: first, the precise meaning of the terms used in explaining Christ's position in relation to God and his creation, and second, the nature of the heresy that Paul seems to be warning the Colossians to avoid. We shall try to deal with both of these issues as we go through the letter. Here is a plan of the letter.

1. *Introduction*
(1.1–2)  Greetings from Paul and Timothy.
(1.3–11) We thank God for your advancement in the faith, which Epaphras has told us about, and we pray for you to continue to progress.
(1.12–14) Thank God for saving you from the power of darkness through the sacrifice of his Son.

2. *Christ, the image of the unseen God*
(1.15)  1  He is the image of God and first-born of all creation.
(1.16)  2  Everything in heaven and earth was made by, through and for him.
(1.17)  3  He existed before all things and everything exists in him.

(1.18) 4 He is the head of his body, the church, he is the beginning, the first to be born from the dead.

(1.19) 5 He contains the fullness of God

(1.20) 6 He has reconciled all things to him through his death on the cross.

### 3. *How this applies to you and my relationship with you*

(1.21-23) You, too, have been saved by Christ's sacrifice; keep to the gospel as you first heard it.

(1.24-29; 2.1-8) I am glad to suffer for you. God made me a special minister to reveal to you and other Gentiles his plan of salvation and I am anxious to keep you rooted in Christ. Beware of false teaching.

### 4. *Christ is all-sufficient*

(2.9-15) Christ is the complete fullness of God, so you are complete in him. You have received through him a spiritual circumcision. You have been buried with him in baptism and raised again with him from the dead. The indictment against you has been cancelled. He is triumphant over all authorities.

(2.16-23) Do not take on those old commandments. They are useless. Keep hold of Christ, the head of the body of which you are the parts.

### 5. *The new man in Christ*

(3.1-4) You have died to the world. Your life is with Christ. Set your minds on heaven, not earth.

(3.5-25; 4.1-6) Avoid your old sins and live like the chosen ones of God. Love one another and encourage one another. Special messages for wives, husbands, children, fathers, slaves and masters. Continue in prayer and thanksgiving. By the way, pray for me to say the right things at my trial. Watch your conversation with non-Christians.

### 6. *Final words and signing off*

(4.7-18) Tychicus and Onesimus will inform you about my

situation. Aristarchus, Marcus, Jesus/Justus, Epaphras, Luke and Demas send their regards. Give our regards to the church in Laodicaea and to Nymphas, and to Archippus. Grace be with you.

## 2. Ephesians

Reading Ephesians is rather like climbing a high mountain in cloudy weather. Occasionally the clouds clear and you can glimpse a snowy summit outlined against a blue sky. Then the mist swirls in and you go back to toiling upwards on a rocky path. There is none of the *relative* clarity (since Paul is often difficult to follow compared with other writers) of letters with one major theme such as Galatians. The author packs so many ideas into a passage that we have the task of disentangling the several strands of argument. This is one of the reasons why it is difficult at first to detect the central theme. As Chrysostom's comment above implies, the writer is also attempting to use ordinary language to convey extraordinary ideas. Jerome comments that 'no letter of Paul has such great mysteries (*tanta mysteria*) wrapped up in such abstruse meanings'. The vocabulary is that of a writer who is straining to say something for which no human words are appropriate. Terms such as 'fullness', 'richness' and 'super-abundance', which are used by our writer to convey particular qualities of God, are not easy to explain. It is as though we are at the birth of a new way of thinking, a leap forward in the evolution of the human understanding.

Another reason why the theme is not always immediately clear is the way that a statement can often carry more than one meaning. This is an important feature of this letter and, indeed, of other letters in the NT, where the mind of the rabbi is at work. We should not be looking for the one meaning that will enable us to discard the other possible meanings but rather be open to the idea that more than one meaning is valid. To quote from a recent publication by Jonathan

Magonet,[3] when the schools of the rabbis Hillel and Shammai disagreed on a particular point, a heavenly voice proclaimed: 'Both these and these are the words of the living God!' In other words, our attitude to determining the meaning should be not 'either . . . or' but 'both . . . and'. There are good examples of this phenomenon of several layers of meaning in 2.11–16.

The first chapter sets the tone of the letter and we can sense immediately the heightened emotion indicated by a disregard for the normal rules of good style and grammar and the mantra-like repetition of certain phrases such as 'to the praise of his glory' or 'according to his good pleasure'. These phrases are similar to the 'short praise formulae', the pious phrases known in Judaism as *berakoth*. Incidentally, we should point out that the repetition of the preposition **en**, 'in', which occurs twenty-six times in the twenty-three verses of the first chapter, might at first sight strike one as unusual, but we find the same repetition in other letters such as Romans. The writer does not resort to the standard expressions of Platonism or Stoicism or the familiar concepts that we find used by non-Christian philosophers of the period writing on theological matters. His distinctive approach can be illustrated by v.19, where we have four related nouns used to describe the way God acts in his church: 'power', 'action', 'might' and 'strength'. This gives an impression of awkward repetition, as though the author is trying to find the correct word by listing all the possible terms that might apply to God. It is only when we examine them in detail that we begin to appreciate the profundity of the writer's theme. Let us start with a plan of the structure of the letter.

1. *Introduction*
(1.1–2) Greetings.
(1.3–14) Praised be God for the blessings he has given us

---

[3] *The Subversive Bible*, SCM Press 1997, p. 106.

through Christ and for deciding that both we Jews and you Gentiles should receive an everlasting inheritance and the gift of the Holy Spirit.

### 2. *My prayer for you*
(1.15–19) Thanks be to God for your faith and love. May you learn more fully how marvellous is the inheritance awaiting us and what power God has.

### 3. *The power of God*
(1.20–23) God has shown his power in raising Jesus from the dead and appointing him as the head of the church.
(2.1–6) God has also shown his power by raising us from death, the death of sin, and allowing us to sit in heaven with Christ.

### 4. *The grace of God*
(2.7–10) All this is a free gift from God. It is not something we have done ourselves.

### 5. *Gentiles and Jews together in Christ*
(2.11–19) In the past you Gentiles had no hope of inheriting the promise, but now Christ has broken down the barrier that separated you from Israel by abolishing the Law's demands through his death on the cross. Through him we all have access to the Father in one Spirit as fellow-citizens.

### 6. *The metaphor of the church as a building*
(2.20–22) We are being built into a holy temple on the foundation of the apostles and prophets, with Christ as the corner-stone.

### 7. *Paul's special mission towards the Gentiles*
(3.1–13) I am in prison because of you. Remember the story of how I was called to preach to the Gentiles. The great secret that the Gentiles are also called to inherit the kingdom of God was

revealed to me. Do not despair at my sufferings on your behalf – you should be proud of them.

### 8. *Paul prays to God for the Gentiles*

(3.14–21) I kneel before God the Father and ask him to give you strength and power, and pray that Christ may dwell in you and that you may know his love. Glory be to God!

### 9. *Unity in the church*

(4.1–6) Behave in a way worthy of your calling, with tolerance and love. Keep the unity of the Spirit in peace. Unity is the keynote of our faith.

(4.7–16) We have all been given grace according to an individual dispensation from Christ. By ascending into Heaven and descending into Hades, he has 'filled all things'. He has appointed various officers to build up the body of Christ, which is the church. He is the Head. We should mature and grow – not be sidetracked by wrong doctrines like children. Christ as the Head of the body supplies each individual part with what it needs for growth.

### 10. *Avoid the pagan way of life*

(4.17–32; 5.1–20) The pagans are corrupt. Do not imitate them. Christ has taught you a new way of life. Do not lie, display anger, or cheat. Watch what you say. Be kind to one another. Imitate God your Father as his children. Avoid sexual sins and outrageous behaviour. Keep away from pagan festivities. They are the work of darkness and you are the children of light. Be on your guard and use your time wisely. Avoid drunkenness. When you meet sing spiritual hymns and songs, thanking God in the name of Jesus.

### 11. *Christian submission*

(5.21–33; 6.1–9) Give way to one another. Marriage provides an allegory of what Christian submission should be like. The headship of the husband over his wife is representative of the headship of Christ over his church. As the church is subject to Christ, wives are subject to their husbands. As Christ loved his church, so should husbands love their wives. Christ sacrificed himself for his church so that she should be a worthy bride for him. Husbands should love their wives because they are their own bodies and wives should respect their husbands. Children should obey their parents and fathers should bring their children up in a Christian way. Slaves should obey their masters as though they were Christ and masters should treat their slaves with kindness. Remember you all have one Master in heaven.

12. *The final exhortation*
(6.10–20) Take the power of the Lord. Put on the armour of God to fight against the devil and wicked powers. Be resolute. Pray at all times and pray for me that I may speak boldly on behalf of the gospel.

13. *Final words and signing off*
(6.21–24) Tychicus will give you all the news about me. Peace and love to you and grace to all who love our Lord Jesus for ever.

## How should this book be used by a group?

This depends on the aims and objectives of the members of the group, but I would like to make the following suggestions:

In the first place, it is not necessary for everyone to be using the same translation of the letters. In fact, if everyone is using the same translation and that translation is compared with the version given in this guide, there may be a tendency to take sides on the issue of which is the better version. If there are several versions being used, this polarization is avoided as people realize there are many valid ways of translating. Someone at least should have the AV, and it helps if someone is following the text in a foreign language. This can frequently give an insight into the meaning that is missed when everyone is using English translations. Secondly, let someone with this guide read aloud the translation given slowly and carefully so that the members of the group can compare it with the translation that they happen to have before them. This should immediately cause questions to arise which can be tackled as the notes are read and explained. Be careful to keep the discussion centred on the meaning of the text.

## A few things to note

1. Certain abbreviations are used throughout this book.

| | |
|---|---|
| AV | Authorised Version |
| NEB | New English Bible |
| NT | New Testament |
| OT | Old Testament |
| Sept. | Septuagint |
| Vulg. | Vulgate (the Latin version of the Bible by St Jerome) |

2. Besides modern writers, whose works are listed at the end of the guide, I have consulted various ancient scholars, most of whom are listed in the biographies below.

## Biographies

**Aristotle,** born in Macedonia (384-322 BC). Student of Plato and tutor to the young Alexander the Great, who founded his own Peripatetic ('Walking around') school of philosophy, at the Lyceum in Athens. Polymath and founder of modern science. Wrote and lectured on many subjects such as logic, ethics, aesthetics, politics, metaphysics and biology. Mediaeval scholasticism was greatly influenced by Aristotle.

**Athanasius** (around 293-373), from Alexandria. At the Council of Nicaea (325) he opposed Arius who argued that the Son and the Father did not share the same substance or essence. Ordained Bishop of Alexandria but had to go into exile when the Arians became the dominant party at court.

**Basil,** 'The Great' (329-79). Educated at Athens and Constantinople. Became Bishop of Caesarea. Supported Athanasius against the Arians. Regarded as the founder of Eastern monasticism. Voluminous writer on most theological subjects.

**John Chrysostom,** 'Golden-mouth' (around 349-407). Wrote homilies on Ephesians and Colossians while still in Antioch. Became bishop of Constantinople famous for his preaching. Died in exile after offending the empress Eudoxia.

**Clement of Alexandria** (around 150-215). His writing on Christian subjects was heavily influenced by the humanism of pagan Greek literature. Head of the Catechetical School in Alexandria until the outbreak of persecution under Septimius Severus forced him to leave Alexandria.

**Jerome** (around 345-420). Studied in Rome and spent some time in Constantinople with Gregory of Nazianzus. Settled in Bethlehem, where he founded four monastic communities. Attacked Pelagianism. Famous for his translation of the Bible into Latin. Wrote commentaries on Ephesians and Colossians which relied heavily on the missing works of Origen.

**Josephus** (born around 37). Pharisee who took part in the Jewish rebellion against the Romans. Captured in 67, he settled in Rome. Wrote *The Jewish War* and *Antiquities*. Although pro-Roman, he defended the Jewish race and religion against the Alexandrian scholar Apion.

**Novatian** (around 200-258). Founded the schismatic group of

Catharoi, who took a hard line over the reinstatement of repentant defectors. Probably martyred during the reign of the emperor Valerian. Wrote several works, including 'On the Trinity', of which few survive.

**Origen** (around 185-254). Christian Platonist and biblical scholar. His works were used extensively by Jerome when writing his commentaries. Taught first in Alexandria and then Palestine, where he was ordained priest. Imprisoned and tortured during Decian persecutions.

**Pliny (the Younger)** (around 61-113). Governor of Bithynia, where he had cause to ask the advice of the emperor Trajan about his policy towards Christianity. Famous for his letters and his eye-witness account of the eruption of Vesuvius.

**Strabo** (around 63 BC - AD 21). Geographer and historian from Pontus. His *Geography* in seventeen volumes has survived, but we do not have his *Historical Sketches*.

**Tertullian** (around 160-225). Trained as a lawyer. Spent most of his life in Carthage. Most important for his ability to express Christian terms in Latin. Defended Christianity against pagans and Jews and expounded Christian doctrine and practice in the church. Later joined the strict Montanist sect.

**Theodoret** (around 393-457). Taught by Chrysostom and Theodore. Bishop of Cyrrhus near Antioch. Involved in controversy against the Monophysites. Wrote a continuation of Eusebius' *History of the Church* and concise notes on New Testament letters.

**Theophylact** (latter part of eleventh century). Archbishop of Acris in Bulgaria. His commentaries on Paul's letters owe a great deal to Chrysostom.

# The Letter to the Colossians

## Chapter 1

1 Paul, an apostle of Christ Jesus through the will of God, and Timothy our brother 2 [send greetings] to the saints in Colossae and to the faithful brothers and sisters in Christ. Grace to you and peace from God our Father. 3 We thank God the Father of our Lord Jesus Christ at all times when we pray for you, 4 having heard of your faith in Christ Jesus and the love you show towards all the saints,

[1] Timothy is associated with Paul in writing this letter, although he is not mentioned in the letter to the Ephesians. Was he mentioned here because he was known to the Colossians but not to the recipients of the other letter, whoever they were? Was he absent when Ephesians was written? These may be interesting questions but we do not know the answers. We need not see anything sinister in this, as similar questions can be asked about Timothy's absence from the letter to the Galatians, although he is mentioned in both letters to the Corinthians and in Romans, letters which must have been written about the same time as Galatians, a letter which is universally attributed to Paul.

[2] 'Faithful . . . in Christ' can be taken in the sense of 'the Christian faithful'. I hesitate, however, to translate it as 'believing in Christ', since there is no clear example in the NT

of **pistos en** meaning 'believing in', although the noun **pistis**, 'belief', followed by **en** can mean 'belief in', as we see in v. 4. From its position in the sentence, this phrase seems to refer to others who are not in Colossae, although the AV, 'To the saints and faithful brethren in Christ which are at Coloss[a]e', is also acceptable. Nevertheless, the Greek word order would indicate that one group is 'the saints in Colossae', and the second group 'the faithful brothers and sisters' elsewhere. The absence of a definite article with the second group is not important, since Paul's use of the article is inconsistent, and as he may be intending to refer to 'any others', not just a specific group, the absence of the article is reasonable. This reference to another group makes sense if we remember that this letter was intended to be read out to the Laodicaeans as described in 4.16. The same distinction between two groups is clearer in the opening verse of Ephesians, where 'who are' is added before 'in Ephesus'.

'From God our Father' in Paul's letters normally continues 'and the Lord Jesus Christ'. Several manuscripts add the phrase

[3] 'We thank', i.e. Paul and Timothy. There is no need to regard the 'we' as an author's plural.

[4] 'Faith in Christ Jesus', **pistin en Christôi Iêsou,** is a common phrase in Paul. See my notes on Gal. 2.16 in *Reading Through Galatians*.

'Show', **echete,** literally 'have'.

Note 'faith' and 'love'; 'hope' appears in the next verse to complete the famous trinity of I Cor. 13.13.

5 because of the hope laid up for you in heaven, which you heard about before in the word of truth, the gospel, 6 which is there with you, just as it is in all the world, bearing fruit and increasing, as it is also among you, from the day you heard it and recognized the

grace of God in truth, 7 just as you learned it from
Epaphras our beloved fellow-slave, who is Christ's
faithful servant on our behalf, 8 the one who also
revealed to us your love in the Spirit.

[5] Paul continues the long, rambling sentence which he
started in v. 3 and which he will finally end in v. 8. The style is
typically unpolished, with three clauses introduced by **kathôs**,
'[just] as'.

'Because of the hope' indicates the reason both for the faith
that inspires them and for the love they show to others. It is not
the reason for the earlier statement 'we thank God'. We may be
surprised that faith and love are seen as dependent on hope.
Our modern obsession with altruism makes us uneasy with the
idea that Christians may be motivated by the hope of eternal
life or the future inheritance promised to believers in Christ.
See my notes on Heb. 10.35, 36 in *Reading Through Hebrews*.

'You heard about *before*', **proêkousate**, is a subtle way of
reminding them that the original gospel they heard was the
correct one and that the new versions they are getting from
false teachers are to be rejected. The addition of the phrase 'in
the word of truth' presses this point home.

[6] 'Bearing fruit', **karpophoroumenon**, refers to the increase
in good deeds; 'increasing', **auxanomenon**, to the growth in
numbers of converts.

'As it is in all the world' should not be taken as meaning that
the gospel has already reached every corner of the world but
that it is spreading everywhere.

[7] Epaphras is probably an abbreviation for Epaphroditus, a
name derived from the goddess Aphrodite. An Epaphroditus is
named in Phil. 2.25; 4.18. There are quite a few names ending
in -as which appear to be abbreviations, such as Loukas, i.e.
Luke, probably short for Lucanus, Demas, Hermas, Artemas

and, if this is the correct form of the nominative of the name occurring in 4.15, Nymphas. The pagan origin of some of these names is clear. Perhaps in their abbreviated form they were more acceptable.

Epaphras clearly was Paul's main link with the church in Colossae, since he had been its founder and kept Paul informed of its development.

'On our behalf', **hyper hêmôn,** is better supported than 'on your behalf', **hyper hûmôn,** the reading of some manuscripts. The two pronouns are frequently confused.

[8] 'In the Spirit', **en pneumati,** has no definite article. This is not an argument for taking **pneumati** as not referring to *the* Holy Spirit, since Paul, as I have pointed out before, is inconsistent in his use of the definite article. But it is also possible to translate the phrase as 'spiritual', i.e. as opposed to 'fleshly'.

9 Because of this, since the day we heard [of it], we, too, have not stopped praying for you and asking that you be filled with the knowledge of his will in all wisdom and spiritual insight, 10 to walk worthily of the Lord to his complete pleasure, fruitful in every good work and growing in the knowledge of God, 11 empowered with all power according to the might of his glory for total endurance and joyful long-suffering,

[9] 'This', in 'because of *this*', most probably refers to the good report of their progress that Paul had received from Epaphras. It is possible, however, that it refers to the original conversion of the Colossians.

'Knowledge', **epignôsin,** is repeated in the next verse. Its cognate verb, which I translate as 'recognized', **epegnôte,** occurs in v. 6. We should not assume that because the noun is used four times in Colossians Paul is contrasting true knowledge with the false knowledge of *Gnost*icism. If he were making such an allusion, he would probably have used the more obvious noun, **gnôsis**, itself rather than the compound **epignôsis**. In fact, **gnôsis** only occurs once in Colossians. **Epignôsis** can denote either the process of 'getting to know' or 'recognition'. There has been a tendency among modern commentators to assume that the heresy he is warning the Colossians against was some form of early Gnostic doctrine, but we have no evidence for this.

'Wisdom and spiritual insight', **sophiâi kai synesei pneumatikêi**, are the manifestations of the knowledge of God's will; they are the result of 'getting to know' God. In Eph. 1.8 wisdom is coupled with 'judgment', **phronêsei**. **Synesis**, which can also be translated as 'understanding' or 'comprehension', is described by Aristotle (*Nicomachean Ethics*, 1143a, 10) as 'capable of discerning', **kritikê**, and contrasted with the more pragmatic faculty of **phronêsis**. It is interesting that **sophiâ**, **synesis** and **phronêsis** are described together by Aristotle (*Nicomachean Ethics*, 1103a, 5) as virtues of the thinking faculty. See also the notes on Eph. 1.8, 17.

[10] 'Fruitful', **karpophorountes**, and 'growing', **auxanomenoi**, echo v. 6.

[11] 'Empowered' is used with 'power' to show that the Greek terms are also related, i.e. **dynamoumenoi** and **dynamei**.

'Might of his glory', **kratos tês doxês autou**, probably means the same as 'his glorious might'. For the meaning of **kratos**, see the notes on Eph. 1.19.

'Total endurance', **pâsan hypomonên**, (AV) 'all patience'.

'Joyful', **meta charâs**, literally 'with joy', has been taken by some commentators with the verb 'thanking' in the next verse, but the paradox of 'joyful long-suffering' is not as strong in Greek as it is in translation, since the Greek word **makrothûmiân**, literally, is 'long temper'. Furthermore, it is typical of Paul to end a clause with a prepositional phrase. The same sentiment, incidentally, is found in James 1.2–3, 'Think it all *joy*, (**charân**), my brothers and sisters, when you meet with various trials, knowing that the testing of your faith produces *patience* (**hypomonên**).'

12 thanking the Father who qualified you to share in the lot of the saints in the light; 13 who rescued us from the power of darkness and transported us to the kingdom of his dear son, 14 in whom we have our redemption, the forgiveness of our sins,

[12] 'Qualified', **hikanôsanti**, literally, 'made sufficient'.

'Lot', **klêrou**, for the more usual 'inheritance', **klêronomiâs**.

'The saints in the light' should not be taken as referring to the departed saints, although they obviously are not excluded from that light, but as describing the present state of all the faithful. The reference to the future implicit in the AV's use of the term 'inheritance' to translate **klêrou** can mislead the reader into thinking that 'in the light', **en tôi phôti**, refers to a future state, but it is important to note that 'illuminated', **phôtismenoi**, is a synonym for 'baptized', not 'departed and gone to heaven'. The contrast between light and darkness is also to be seen in Eph. 5.8, 9. See also the notes on v. 14 of the same chapter.

[13] 'Rescued', **errhûsato**, is also found in the Lord's Prayer in the phrase 'deliver (**rhûsai**) us from evil'. As 'evil' in the prayer should really be translated as 'the evil one', the parallel is obvious.

'Power (or authority) of darkness', **exousiâs tou skotous**, is probably Satan, not the 'world-masters of this darkness' of Eph. 6.12. See the notes on that verse.

'Transported us to the kingdom' is more than a metaphor. See my notes on Eph. 1.3 and 2.6, and on Heb. 12.22 in *Reading Through Hebrews*. We have in some profound sense already been taken up to heaven by Christ. It may seem to contradict the statement in v. 5 that we have a 'hope laid up in heaven', in other words, that we are not yet in full possession of our inheritance, but this paradox is one we have to accept.

'Of his dear son', **tou huiou tês agapês autou,** literally, 'of the son of his love'.

[14] This verse is repeated, with additions and a slight variation in vocabulary, in Eph. 1.7.

'Redemption', **apolytrôsin,** is release (from captivity) on the payment of a ransom. Payment is a core part of redemption for Paul. The payment is not mentioned here, but it is in Eph. 1.7. Compare I Cor. 6.20; 7.23, 'You have been bought at a price'.

'Of our sins', **tôn hamartiôn,** varies from **tôn paraptômatôn** of Ephesians. These two terms are synonyms, as I point out in more detail in my notes on Eph. 2.1.

15 who is the image of the unseen God, first-born of all creation, 16 for in him was created everything in heaven and on earth, seen and unseen, whether thrones or powers, whether rulers or authorities; everything has been created through him and to end in him.

[15–18] These verses are often described in modern commentaries as a 'hymn'. Since they have no metrical pattern, special vocabulary or anything one might associate with verse, I prefer to treat them as prose. They are the deep meditations of a mind attempting to express something inexpressible, but the fact that they contain the most profound and moving thoughts still does not make them verse. Some modern translations give the illusion that this passage is verse by laying it out on the page in stanzas, which commentators such as Martin describe as 'strophes', but it is still prose.

[15] 'Image', **eikôn**, is a difficult word. Because Christ was the 'image', literally, 'likeness', of God, we should not assume that meant he could not be God. **Eikôn** can denote more than similarity between two objects; it can indicate a shared identity. The word is also used in Platonist writings to denote the 'Form' or 'Ideal' from which are derived the material copies of objects in the world of the senses. In this sense Christ was the 'form' of which Adam is a copy. See my notes on Heb. 10.1 in *Reading Through Hebrews*.

'Of the unseen God' is a phrase full of meaning. Adam was made in the image of God, as we read in Gen. 1.26 (Sept.), 'and God said, "Let us make man *according to our image*, **kat'eikona hêmeterân**"'. So firstly, as Christ is the *visible* image of God made flesh, Adam was made like him, visible and material. Secondly, since Christ is the image of the *invisible*, his likeness to God cannot be expressed in material terms. His relationship with the Father is a spiritual one.

'First-born' was seized upon by the Arians, who saw in the term an admission that there was a time when Christ did not exist. In Judaism, however, the title is an honorary one, seniority implying superiority. It is also a title associated with the Messiah, as we see in Ps. 89.27 (Sept. 88.28), 'and I will appoint him my *first-born* (**prôtotokon**), high above the kings of the earth'. Lightfoot paraphrases the phrase 'first-born of all creation' as 'sovereign Lord over all creation by virtue of primogeniture'. See my notes on the meaning of this word in Heb. 1.6 in *Reading Through Hebrews*. The difficulty of this word is increased by the addition of the phrase 'of all creation', **pâsês ktiseôs**, which can also mean 'of every creature', as the AV puts it. Various suggestions have been made:

1. 'first to be born *before* all creation';
2. 'the first-born *who was sacrificed for* all creation';
3. 'the first-born of the *new* creation';
4. 'the first *father* of all creation', i.e. 'fathering the creation as his first-born'.

Of the above, the fourth is a rare meaning, although grammatically possible, and is far removed from any normal NT concept of Christ, the third must be rejected because it would require the addition of the word 'new' in the text, and the second, although subtle and doctrinally sound, would also require the addition of 'who was sacrificed for' and so is unlikely to be the meaning here. The first suggestion is the closest to the correct meaning, but it is still not quite right, since we can hardly extract 'before' from the wording, and, more seriously, because it implies that Christ had also been created, even it if it was before anything else. It is much more reasonable to take this phrase as meaning that because Christ entered into a creation which had come about through his agency, and became part of it himself as a means of redeeming it, he is in a special sense 'the first-born' of that creation. In other words, on his incarnation Christ was the superior of his creation, the first-born who would inherit all that his Father had made. Nevertheless, as this was part of the plan made by God before time began, Christ was already the first-born even before his incarnation. The Son is Son from eternity. As we read below in v. 17, 'he has been in existence before everything'; he was not created, hence no explanation of the phrase 'first-born of all creation' which implies that he *was* created can be valid, since it would be inconsistent with the rest of this passage.

[16] 'In him', **en autôi**, or 'by him'. See the notes in *Reading Through Galatians* on Gal. 1.6 regarding the ambiguity of **en**.

In the parallel passage, Eph. 1.21, **dynameôs**, 'power', takes the place of 'thrones', **thronoi**, a word not found in Ephesians. See my notes on that passage. Although clearly related passages, they make different points. Here the 'powers' are seen as subordinate because they were created in/by Christ; in the Ephesians passage they were made subject to Christ when he was raised from the dead.

'Through him', **di'autou**, emphasizes Christ's function as the agent through whom God acts. **En** stresses his instrumentality, i.e. the means by which God worked.

'To end in him', **eis auton**, literally, 'to/into him'. As Christ begins creation, so creation is to be finally restored by returning to him. He is the purpose for which things were made. See the note on 'sum up' in Eph. 1.10. The AV's 'for him' gives the impression that the world was created for his sake, as a sort of gift or a compliment. The Vulgate has *in ipso*, 'in himself', for both **en autôi** at the start of the verse and **eis auton**.

Note 'was created', **ektisthê**, and 'has been created', **ektistai**. The change from the historic aorist to the perfect is deliberate. The original creation is described as an event in the past, but having been created it is now perceived as continuing to exist in Christ. 'Has been created' has the sub-text 'and still exists'. It also leads logically to the statement in the next verse, 'everything exists in him'.

17 And he himself has been in existence before everything, and everything exists in him, 18 and he himself is the head of his body, the church, the beginning, first-born from the dead, so that he himself might be first in everything,

[17] 'Has been in existence', actually, 'is', **estin**. John 8.58 makes the same point, 'Before Abraham was, *I am* (**egô eimi**)', or, to put it in a more modern idiom, '*I have been in existence since before Abraham was born*'. Greek uses the present in cases where English would use a special tense not found in many languages. For example, 'I have been waiting for some time' in English means 'I started to wait some time ago and am still waiting'. In Greek, or French, for example, one would say 'I wait for some time'. So 'has been in existence' implies that he existed in the past and still exists.

'Before', **pro**, can have a temporal or a hierarchical sense. In other words, Christ was already existing before the creation of the world, and also he was superior to everything else.

'Exists in him', **en autôi synestêken**, literally, 'stands together in him', or 'has been put together by him', Vulg. *in ipso constant*. Aristotle (*Nicomachean Ethics*, 1141b, 1) speaks of the elements 'out of which the **kosmos** *has been composed*, **synestêken**'. The double meaning of this verb is appropriate. Not only was everything created in the past through Christ, it is also kept together by him now. 'Together', **syn-**, also hints that the universe is a unity. Note also the repetition of 'himself', **autos**, in this and the next verse.

[18] The parallel passage Eph. 1.22, 23, 'and "he has subjected all things beneath his feet" and given him as head above all things to the church, which is his body', adds the point that God the Father is the agent in this process.

'Head' is a complex metaphor; the head is in a position of supremacy over the rest of the body, but at the same time it is part of the body. It needs the body in order to form a whole person, as the Ephesians passage makes clear. Furthermore, the head is, as Lightfoot says, 'the centre of vital force, the source of all energy and life'.

'Beginning', **archê**, a word that also means 'rule', but not here. Martin draws attention to the link with Gen. 1.1 (Sept.), '*In the beginning*, **en archêi**, God created heaven and earth', and Prov. 8.22, 'The Lord made me the *beginning*, **archên**, of his ways for his works'. The latter text is particularly appropriate when we look at the rest of the passage, the subject of which is Wisdom, for example, v. 27 (AV), 'When he prepared the heavens, I was there', and v. 30, 'Then I was by him, as one brought up with him: and I was daily his delight, rejoicing always before him'. It is very likely that the early church used these verses to prove the pre-existence of Christ.

'First-born from the dead' echoes v. 15, 'first-born of all creation'. The connection between these two phrases is that just as Christ initiated the redemption by entering into the world that he had created, so he leads the way in the resurrection from the dead.

'First', **prôteuôn,** not just **prôtos,** the normal word for 'first'. **Prôteuôn,** literally 'holding first place', refers not only to coming first in time, but also to being pre-eminent or outstanding. Just as an athlete arrives first at the tape, so he also wins first prize. Similarly, 'in everything', **en pâsin,** can mean either 'in all things' or 'among all people'.

19 because all the fullness was content to dwell in him, 20 and through him to reconcile to him again all things, whether on earth or in heaven, having made peace through him, through the blood of his cross.

[19] 'Fullness', **plêrôma,** is used seventeen times in the NT, nearly always in the sense of 'fullness' or 'fulfilment'. Its use in Matt. 9.16 and Mark 2.21 to denote a patch in a garment is simply an extension of its basic meaning , i.e. 'something that fills in a gap'. Here it refers to the full complement of divinity which is shared by the Son. It is all that makes God complete, the sum total of all his glory, might and love. In Eph.1.23 the **plêrôma** refers to the church, but that passage is making a totally different point. See my notes on Eph. 1.23 and 3.19. Many commentators try to see a connection between the use of **plêrôma** in Colossians and Ephesians and the Gnostic use of this word to denote an **aiôn** which has become incarnate in Christ. There is no need to suppose that Paul is attacking Gnosticism specifically in this verse; it is more likely that he is attacking both the objections of monotheistic Judaism to the divinity of Christ and the claims of polytheistic paganism that other gods shared divinity with him. Lightfoot's commentary, incidentally, has a useful appendix on **plêrôma.**

I take the subject of the verb 'was content', **eudokêsen,** as the **plêrôma,** in effect, God himself. It is possible to make Christ the subject, 'he was content that all the fullness should dwell in him', but if we do, the pronouns in the next verse present problems.

[20] 'Through him', **di'autou**, clearly refers to Christ; 'to him', **eis auton**, should refer to the Father, who is implied in the reference to 'the fullness' of the previous verse. If we took Christ as the subject of 'was content' in the previous verse, it is hard to accept **eis auton** as referring to the Father, since we did not take him as the subject of that verse, and hence he has not been mentioned; one would have expected a reference to 'God' or 'Father', as indeed we have in the parallel reference in Eph. 2.16, where Christ is described as the one who does the reconciling. Since Paul is lax in his usage of the third person reflexive, we cannot use the lack of the reflexive, 'to himself', **eis heauton**, as an argument in identifying the one to whom he is referring.

'To reconcile . . . again', **apokatallaxai**, not just 'to reconcile', which is **katallaxai**. The longer compound is only found in Colossians and Ephesians; the shorter word is found in Romans and I and II Corinthians. It may be that Paul is treating the verbs as synonyms, but it is highly probable that he is making a new doctrinal point, i.e. that the reconciliation between God and mankind which was caused by Christ's sacrifice restored an original state of harmony. We were not always enemies of God. I assume that the Father is the one who reconciles us to him through Christ, as he clearly is in II Cor. 5.18 and 19. The latter is particularly appropriate, 'for God was in Christ reconciling the world to himself'. As I have already pointed out, Eph 2.16 makes Christ the reconciler, but this is not a significant variation, since in v. 22 below he could also be the subject of the verb 'he has reconciled again'.

'Having made peace', **eirênopoiêsâs**, a verb only found here in the NT, is strictly speaking ungrammatical, being masculine and not neuter, as it should be, to agree with **plêrôma**. As, however, the **plêrôma** is God, the shift in gender is acceptable. Ephesians 2.15 has Christ, not the Father, 'making peace', **poiôn eirênên**, but that is because Christ is also referred to as the reconciler.

The repetition of the phrase 'through him' and the use of **dia**, 'through', three times in one verse obviously disturbed some scribes, because some manuscripts omit the second occurrence of 'through him'. Nevertheless, the best manuscripts keep it. The repetition may be stylistically unattractive, but it is typical of Paul, who is clearly emphasizing the part played by Christ in God's plan of salvation.

21 And you, who were once excluded and hostile in your thinking and your wicked deeds, 22 he has now reconciled again in the body of his flesh through his death, to present you as holy, blameless and free from reproach before his face, 23 that is, indeed, if you remain firmly founded in the faith and do not shift from the hope of the gospel, which you heard and which was proclaimed in the whole of creation under heaven, the gospel of which I, Paul, was made a servant.

[21] 'Excluded', **apêllotriômenous**, as we can see from its occurrence in Eph. 2.12 and 4.18, is a more accurate translation than 'alienated', which nowadays tends to mean emotionally 'estranged'. The meaning is that they were literally treated as foreigners or aliens, being Gentiles without the Law and without the promises of the covenant. The Ephesians version (2.12), as usual, spells this out more clearly.

'Hostile', **echthrous**, both to the Jews and to God, as we see from Eph. 2.14, which speaks of Christ destroying the 'hostility', **echthrân**, symbolized by the barrier in the Temple at Jerusalem which kept the Gentiles outside the Court of Israel. See the notes on that verse.

[22] 'Reconciled again', **apokatêllaxen:** the subject is either God, as above, or Christ, as in Eph. 2.16. See notes on v. 20.

'In the body of his flesh', **en tôi sômati tês sarkos autou**, is split in Ephesians into two separate references: 2.14, 'by his flesh', and 2.16, 'in one body'. But there can be little doubt that the same message is intended. The reference to 'flesh' has at least two meanings: it refers, firstly, to the incarnation, and secondly, to the sacrifice on the cross. We can also add that it may refer to the sacramental eating of Christ's flesh, a ritual which expresses openly the unity of the church. 'In the body' also has more than one meaning: again the incarnation and the sacrifice on the cross are referred to, but it is also an allusion to the body of the church, an allusion made clearer in Eph. 2.16. The link between the church and the sacrifice on the cross is 'through his death', since it is only when we die with Christ that we can be presented to God as an acceptable sacrifice. See my notes on Eph. 2.16 for a fuller exposition. Before leaving this topic, it is worth pointing out that the phrase 'in the body of his flesh', although it reminds one of the Hebrew expression 'his body of flesh', which is simply 'his physical body', means a great deal more than that.

'Holy, blameless' is echoed in Eph. 1.4. 'Blameless', **amômous**, is the word used in the Sept. to refer to the sacrificial animals required by the Mosaic Law, and stands for the Hebrew expression translated in the AV by 'without blemish'; it is found frequently, as here, in association with the word 'holy', **hagios**, in the same context. In other words, the faithful believer is seen as a sacrifice offered to God. This is spelled out in Rom. 12.1, ' So I beseech you, brothers and sisters, by the mercy of God, to present your bodies as a living, holy sacrifice, well-pleasing to God', and Rom. 15.16, 'that the offering of the Gentiles should be well received, sanctified by the Holy Spirit'. There can be little doubt that the sacrifice of the believer is seen as following the pattern of Christ's sacrifice on the cross.

'Before his face', **katenôpion autou**, refers to God the Father, as in Eph. 1.4. The notion that Christ takes us and introduces us to God is found in Eph. 2.18. There is a double image here, the presentation of a sacrifice on the altar, and the presentation of envoys or suppliants in the court of a powerful king.

[23] 'That is, indeed, if', **ei ge**, an expression which in the NT is only used by Paul, and usually in an ironic sense: 'if, indeed – and, of course, you *do* remain firm.' See Eph. 3.2 and Gal. 3.4 for similar uses of **ei ge**.

'Firmly founded', **tethemeliômenoi kai hedraioi**, literally, 'founded and steadfast', a building metaphor elaborated in Eph. 2.20. The noun **themelios**, 'foundation', occurs in the latter passage and also in Rom. 15.20; I Cor. 3.10–12; I Tim. 6.19 and II Tim. 2.19. The participle **tethemeliômenoi** also occurs in Eph. 3.17, where I translate it as 'grounded'.

'Hope of the gospel', i.e. the hope given to you by the gospel.

'In the whole of creation' should not be taken too literally. As in v.6, Paul means that the gospel is spreading everywhere, not that it has already reached every part of creation.


24 Now I am glad to suffer for you, and in compensation I am making up for the shortfall of Christ's tribulations in my flesh for his body's sake, namely, the church, 25 of which I have been made a servant following the stewardship of God assigned to me over you, that is, to proclaim fully the word of God, 26 the secret hidden away from past ages and generations, but now revealed to his saints,


[24] 'I am glad to suffer', literally, 'I rejoice at the sufferings'.

'In compensation I am making up for' is one word in Greek, a word found nowhere else in the NT: **antanaplêrô**, literally, 'I fill up in return'.

'The shortfall', **ta hysterêmata**, literally, 'the things that are missing'.

This is a difficult verse to follow. We can start by rejecting the notion that Christ's sufferings were insufficient, and that the deficiency had to be made up by others. The deficiency of suffering is Paul's. First, because of the suffering which Paul as an individual had inflicted on the church, and which, in another, more profound, sense, he had inflicted on Christ himself, by persecuting the church before his conversion, Paul owed a debt of suffering. Chrysostom, Theophylact and Augustine all support the idea that Christ suffers in his church, because it is his body. Commenting on Ps. 61, Augustine says of Christ, 'he suffers in his members, that is, in ourselves.' Secondly, Paul shared the joint responsibility of all sinful human beings for Christ's sufferings on behalf of fallen humanity. 'The shortfall of Christ's tribulations in my flesh' is a condensed way of saying 'the shortfall of sufferings which my flesh should endure for the sufferings of Christ caused by me'. To put it crudely, the balance sheet showed that Paul had not suffered enough to compensate for the sufferings he had inflicted on Christ. Of course, Paul could not pay off his debt; he would never imagine that he could. He knew that he was saved by grace, not for any merits earned by his sufferings. So we should not assume that Paul is claiming that he can literally pay off his debt.

There are other interpretations of this passage. One is that Christ's sufferings are shared by all Christians, so the shortfall is the suffering which they still have to endure; another related view is that there is a quota of suffering which has to be endured before the end. Both interpretations are sometimes combined. It is certainly true that Christians are called to share the sufferings of Christ. See I Peter 2.19–21, for instance. Nevertheless, such interpretations do not quite fit the context of this verse, which specifically refers to Paul's relationship with the church. Paul speaks of his suffering, not just as the lot of any Christian, but as a particular need arising from his connection with the body of Christ which he persecuted, and in whose service Christ appointed him as an apostle.

[25] 'Following the stewardship', **kata tên oikonomiân**, a word which occurs nine times in the NT. It is used three times in Ephesians and once in Colossians, but not in a sense materially different from its usage elsewhere, i.e. 'management

[of a household]'. The special commission given by God to Paul is referred to again in Eph. 3.2.

'Over you', **eis hûmâs**, literally, '[in]to you'.

'To proclaim fully', **plêrôsai**, literally, 'to complete' or 'to fulfil'. The idea seems to be that the evangelizing of the Gentiles is seen as the fulfilment of the gospel. If it were only the Jews who were allowed to hear the good news, the task could not be completed.

[26] 'The secret', **to mystêrion**, is God's hidden purpose which has now been revealed. Unlike the **mystêria** of pagan cults, which are meant to be kept secret from the uninitiated, Christianity's 'mysteries' are revealed to all following the incarnation, death and resurrection of Christ. One of God's hidden purposes which has been revealed is that the Gentiles too should share in the salvation offered to the Jews by Christ's sacrifice. This seems to be the core meaning of **mystêrion**, which runs through both letters. There is no reason to accept the suggestion that the word **mystêrion** is used in Colossians or Ephesians to convey something different from its normal meaning elsewhere in Paul's letters.

27 to whom God has wished to make known what is the richness of the glory of this secret among the Gentiles, that is, Christ among you, the hope of glory, 28 whom we proclaim as we counsel everyone and teach everyone in all wisdom, in order that we may present everyone perfect in Christ. 29 To this end I toil and strive according to his working that works in me with power.

[27] 'Richness of the glory', **ploutos tês doxês**, is more than 'glorious riches'. The phrase also ocurs in Eph. 1.18 and 3.16 and Rom. 9.23, and refers to the bounty of God's famous generosity. He is glorious because of the wealth of his blessings

he pours upon us. The addition of the phrase 'of this secret' means that God can now share his richness and glory with his saints because he has revealed his secret plan for our redemption.

'Among the Gentiles' has two meanings: firstly, that the gospel is preached among them, and secondly, that the secret which has been revealed is that the Gentiles are also included with the Jews in the promise of redemption.

I have translated 'Christ among you' with 'among' because it is the same preposition, **en**, which is used in the phrase 'among the Gentiles'. It is an abbreviation for 'Christ *is* among you'.

'The hope of glory' signifies that we have not yet been glorified. It is part of our inheritance, as Eph. 1.18 makes clear.

[28] 'Everyone', **panta anthrôpon**, is expressed three times for emphasis. In other words, Gentiles as well as Jews are included in the scheme of redemption.

[29] There is a splendid paradox in this verse: Paul is striving and struggling, but it is God who is working through him. God does the work but it involves human effort. Because Paul gives God the credit for this, he is not boasting when he talks of his own success.

'I toil', **kopiô**, literally, 'I tire myself out'. See Gal. 4.11 and Eph. 4.28 for other examples of the use of this vivid expression.

'And strive', **agônizomenos**, literally, 'contending [for a prize]'. This verb is frequently found in the context of a public competition or sporting event. Also found in 4.12.

'His working that works', **tên energeian autou tên energoumenên**. **Energeia** is activity or work, i.e. power exercised in action. For the verb see the notes on Gal. 2.8 and 5.6 in *Reading Through Galatians*.

# Chapter 2

1 For I want you to know how much I strive for you and those in Laodicaea and all those who have not seen my face in the flesh, 2 so that their hearts may be comforted, being united in love, [and that they may come] to all the richness of complete understanding, to the knowledge of the secret truth of God, [namely] Christ, 3 in whom are hidden all the treasures of wisdom and knowledge.

[1] 'Strive', **agôna echô,** is a synonym for **agônizomai;** see previous verse.

We would have guessed from the reference to Laodicaea, which is mentioned in chapter 4 three times, that this letter was written with the intention that it should be seen by both churches, even if we had not been specifically told so in 4.16. In 4.13 we find Laodicaea associated with Hierapolis, and so it is not unreasonable to assume that both of the letters to Colossae and Laodicaea were also to be read by the church in Hierapolis. Could it be that there was a third letter addressed to the church in Hierapolis, which was designed to be read by those in Laodicaea and Colossae? It is clear, at any rate, that none of these churches had actually been visited by Paul.

[2] 'United', **symbibasthentes,** a verb also used in 2.19 and Eph. 4.16.

'Of complete understanding', **tês plêrophoriâs tês syneseôs**, literally, 'of the completion of understanding', Vulg. *plen-itudinis intellectus*; see note on 1.9. **Plêrophoriâ** tends to be translated by commentators as though it means 'full assur-ance', i.e. 'complete confidence', but its root meaning is 'payment in full' or 'full satisfaction'. It occurs four times in the NT and in each case there is no proof that it carries any psychological overtones. In Heb. 6.11 I translate it as 'fulfil-ment'. The cognate verb **plêrophoreô**, however, does seem to have the sense of 'to give full assurance', 'to convince', in Rom. 4.21 and 14.5 (AV 'fully persuaded'), but this is a secondary and rarer meaning.

'Knowledge', **epignôsin**; see note on 1.9.

Christ is the secret truth of God; in other words, he is what God planned for the redemption of the world.

[3] 'Wisdom', **sophiâs**; see note on Eph. 1.8.

'Knowledge', **gnôseôs**; see note on 1.9 regarding the use of **gnôsis**.


4 I say this so that no one may mislead you with specious arguments. 5 For even though I am absent in the flesh, at least I am with you in spirit, rejoicing when I perceive your discipline and the firmness of your faith in Christ. 6 So since you have received Christ Jesus the Lord, walk in him, 7 rooted and built up in him and being strengthened in the faith, as you have been taught, overflowing with thankfulness.


[4] What is 'this'? Paul's previous claim that Christ provided everything that the Colossians needed. It would appear that certain individuals had been urging them to carry out certain practices or rituals in order to secure God's approval.

'With specious arguments', **en pithanologiâi**, literally, 'in persuasive talk', Vulg. *in subtilitate sermonum*.

[5] 'Discipline', **taxin**, a military word denoting a line of soldiers. Hence it comes to mean 'good order'.

[6] 'Walk in him', **en autôi peripateite**, that is, 'live your lives in accordance with him'.

[7] 'Rooted and built up', **errhizômenoi kai epoikodo-moumenoi**, a mixed metaphor, like that in Eph. 3.17, combining the idea of a living organism, such as a tree, with that of a building.

'In him' could also be 'on him', i.e. as on a foundation.

'Being strengthened', **bebaioumenoi**, a present participle which indicates that this is a continuous process. The same verb occurs in Heb. 13.9, 'for it is good for the heart *to be strengthened* (**bebaiousthai**) by grace, not foods that did not help those who had recourse to them'. The parallel with this passage is striking, since the 'specious arguments' of v. 4 most probably are those of the Judaizers who were pressing the Colossians to observe the Law's commandments regarding food and purification. See the notes on v. 21 below.

'Overflowing', **perisseuontes**, is a favourite verb of Paul, occurring in II Corinthians, for example, ten times.

8 See that no one shanghais you with philosophy and empty tricks, following human tradition, not following Christ but the elemental powers of the world, 9 because it is in him that all the fullness of the godhead dwells bodily, 10 and it is in him that you have been made complete, [in him] who is the head of every ruler and authority.

[8] 'Shanghais', **sûlagôgôn**, is a strong expression, literally, 'seizes as booty and carries off'. 'Shanghai' is rarely used nowadays, but it is just the right word, referring to a practice once prevalent in the nautical world of drugging sailors and shipping them off as crew to Shanghai, figuratively speaking.

'Empty tricks', **kenês apatês**, literally, 'empty deceit', Vulg. *inanem fallaciam.*

'Human tradition', **paradosin tôn anthrôpôn**, must refer to Jewish religious observances, since the expression seems to be a synonym for 'the traditions of our elders'. For example, in Mark 7.8, when the scribes and Pharisees complain that his disciples are not observing the rituals regarding purification, Jesus responds by saying, 'You abandon the commandment of God and hold *the tradition of men* (**tên paradosin tôn anthrôpôn**).'

'The elemental powers of the world', **ta stoicheia tou kosmou**, an expression which also occurs in v. 20, has been discussed at length by many commentators. In Gal. 4.3–5 the meaning of the phrase is clear from the context. Paul, speaking of the former state of the Jews before Christ came into the world, says, 'This is how it was with us – when we were children we were slaves under *the elemental powers of the world* (**ta stoicheia tou kosmou**). But when the time of fulfilment came God sent out his son, born of a woman, born under the Law, in order to redeem those under the Law, so that we might take up our adoption.' The **stoicheia** are the heavenly bodies which determine times and seasons, i.e. the sun, moon and stars. Hence they determined the right days and times for Jewish rituals to take place. Since these heavenly bodies were also gods to the pagans, the Gentiles were also enslaved to them. There is no need to follow Lightfoot's suggestion that these **stoicheia** are 'elementary teaching'. See my notes in *Reading Through Galatians* for a fuller discussion of this topic.

[9] 'The fullness of the godhead', **plêrôma tês theotêtos**, i.e. Christ contains all that God has; he is complete and perfect. As he has all the power of God, we do not need anything, or anyone, else. This reinforces the message of the previous verse that the 'elemental forces' are no substitute for him. They are irrelevant and powerless or, as Gal. 4.9 says, 'feeble and inadequate'.

'Bodily', **sômatikôs,** is interpreted in the following ways:

1. 'in the body', i.e. incarnate;
2. 'in his body', i.e. in the church;
3. 'in reality', i.e. in fact, not seemingly, as Augustine says, *vere non umbratice*;
4. 'as an organized body', i.e. not distributed through a hierarchy of beings;
5. 'in essence'.

The fourth interpretation is too far-fetched, and would not have been understood in this sense without some extra explanation. The third and fifth were popular with some early church scholars and, although plausible, are derived or secondary interpretations. On balance, the first and the second, which supported by Chrysostom, seem equally likely. Christ is fully God, 'all the fullness of the godhead dwells in him', but he is God made flesh. At the same time, the church is his body, and so shares in the fullness of God.


[10] 'Complete', **peplêrômenoi,** picks up **plêrôma** in the previous verse. Christians are made complete and perfect when they remain in Christ, who is complete and perfect. See the notes on Eph. 1.22–23, a passage which explores this idea in more complex detail.

'Ruler and authority', **archês kai exousiâs,** occur together six times in Colossians and Ephesians and in each case seem to denote angelic and supernatural powers, whether good or evil. Paul is making the point that, since Christ is fully God, all spiritual forces are subordinate to him. Just as he is head of the visible church, so he is the head of the unseen hierarchy.


11 And it is in him that you were circumcised with a circumcision not done by hands, but in the stripping off of the body of flesh in Christ's circumcision, 12 buried together with him in that baptism in which you

were also raised together [with him] through your
faith in the action of God who raised him from the
dead, 13 and while you were dead in your sins and
your uncircumcised flesh, he brought you to life
together with him, having forgiven us all our sins.

[11] The circumcision 'not done by hands', **acheiropoiêtôi**, is
by implication contrasted with normal circumcision, i.e. the
rite which, in effect, defined a Jew. Paul is obliquely reminding
his audience of Gentile believers that they do not need to be
circumcised and so do not need to perform those rituals that
were incumbent on those observing the Jewish Law. This is
identical with the main argument of Galatians. As he says in
Gal. 5.3, 'I declare again to every man who is being circumcised
that he is a debtor to perform the whole of the Law', and in 5.6,
'For in Christ Jesus neither circumcision nor un-circumcision
has any power but faith operating through love [does].' As we
have a home 'not made by hands', **acheiropoiêton** (II Cor. 5.1),
i.e. a spiritual or heavenly home which is not in this world, so
here we have been admitted to the spiritual blessings of the new
covenant by a rite that has superseded the old ritual of
circumcision.

'Of the body of flesh', **tou sômatos tou sarkos**, is a better
reading than the text which gave us the AV's 'the body *of the
sins* (**tôn hamartiôn**) of the flesh'. It is likely that 'of the sins'
crept into the text to explain the original phrase. The meaning
of this complex verse is not immediately apparent. There are
two interpretations, both of which seem perfectly valid: firstly,
we 'strip off' the flesh and our former sinful state in baptism by
mystically dying with Christ, and secondly, Christ 'stripped
off' his flesh when he physically died on the cross. So the phrase
'Christ's circumcision' also has two meanings: firstly, it refers
to the spiritual circumcision of baptism which admits us into
Christ's body, the church, when we symbolically leave our old
bodies by dying to sin; secondly, it refers to the historical event

of symbolic circumcision which Christ underwent when he put off the flesh of his physical body on the cross.

[12] '*Buried together with* (**syntaphentes**) him in that baptism' explains and summarizes the previous verse. The **syn-** prefix, 'together with', which I mentioned in the notes on 1.17, is repeated in **synêgerthête**, 'you were raised together with', and in **synezôöpoiêsen**, 'he brought you to life together with' in the next verse. The significance of this repetition of the **syn-** prefix, which also is also found in Eph. 2.6; 3.6 and 4.16, is discussed in the notes on those verses.

'Through your faith in the action of God' is an abbreviated way of saying, 'Through your faith that God could perform the same action in your case as he performed in the case of his son, i.e. raise you from the dead.'

[13] The switch from 'you' to 'us' in the last part of this verse may seem odd, but Paul is in effect saying, '*You* Gentiles have had *your* sins forgiven in the same way that all of *us*, including the Jewish Christians, have had *our* sins forgiven.' Some manuscripts have 'us' for the second 'you', and others have 'you' for the 'us' of the last part of the verse. The pronouns **hêmeis** and **hûmeis** tend to be confused due to their similar pronunciation in the later period.

'Uncircumcised flesh' can be taken two ways: firstly, as Gentiles, you were physically uncircumcised, and secondly, you had not yet received the new spiritual circumcision of baptism.

'*Brought* you *to life together* (**synezôöpoiêsen**) with him', i.e. by baptism. The subject of this verb is God rather than Christ. It is, however, often difficult in Paul's letters to be sure who is the subject in passages where he has been speaking of the Son and the Father.

'Having forgiven', **charisamenos**, from **charizomai**, a verb related to the word for 'grace', **charis**. **Charizomai** has no equivalent in English; it can mean 'give graciously' (as in Gal. 3.18), 'grant a request', 'oblige', 'favour', 'indulge', 'comply', 'give up as a favour', but in Colossians and Ephesians it always carries the meaning 'forgive'. For **charis** see my notes on Gal. 1.3 and Heb. 12.28 in this series of guides.

14 Having cancelled the document against us according to the judgments, [the document] which was not in our favour, he has taken it away, nailing it to the cross. 15 By divesting himself he openly made an example of the rulers and authorities and triumphed over them on it.

[14] 'Having cancelled', **exaleipsâs**, literally, 'having wiped out', a technical term used to describe removing details from a legal document. Grammatically speaking, this participle and its clause go with the previous sentence, since the writer starts a new sentence with '*And* he has taken it away'. It is not clear whether Christ or God is the subject of this new sentence.

'The document against us', **to kath'hêmôn cheirographon**, is a manuscript note which contains a statement witnessing against us, not necessarily an IOU, as Moule suggests, but any legal document which makes an unfavourable declaration about us. It could be regarded either as a statement testifying to our sinfulness or as a bond stating the debt we owe to God.

'According to the judgments', **tois dogmasin**, literally, 'by the decrees'. This is a difficult expression, but the corresponding term in Eph. 2.15 throws some light on it. There we have the expression 'the Law of the commandments *with its decrees* (**en dogmasin**)', which is clearly a reference to the Mosaic Law or *Torah*. So here the meaning must be that, measured against the commandments of the Law, we have failed and so have incurred a penalty which is recorded against us in a legal **cheirographon**. The phrase **tois dogmasin** could possibly also be translated as 'which is in the judgments' or 'which has been recorded as a result of the judgments'. The AV also connects **cheirographon** with **tois dogmasin** and translates 'the handwriting of ordinances that was against us'. There is no justification for accepting the suggestion that the **dogmata** are the doctrines or precepts of the Christian faith, an interpretation widespread among Greek commentators, probably because it reflected a usage current during a later period. Hence we should reject such translations as 'having cancelled *by the precepts* the bond against us'. See also the notes on Eph. 2.15.

'Has taken it away', **êrken ek tou mesou**, literally, 'has lifted up from the middle'.

'Nailing it to the cross' is a graphic way of saying that Christ's sacrifice has cancelled our liability. Perhaps this refers to a method of filing away cancelled or lapsed documents.

[15] This amazing verse is particularly difficult to interpret due to the various layers of meaning lurking beneath the surface. Let us start with the unusual word **apekdûsamenos**, which is only found in this letter. Some commentators, taking 'the rulers and authorities' as the object of this verb, have translated it as 'despoiling', e.g. Vulg. *expolians*. There are, however, no examples of this participle, or its cognate forms **apodûsamenos** and **ekdûsamenos**, taking someone else as the object, i.e. 'despoiling', and in 3.9, the only other place where this verb is found, it must mean 'put off', i.e. 'divest *oneself* of'. So we are left with the question posed by most commentators: is it 'the flesh' or 'the rulers and authorities' that he has stripped off? '*Stripping off* (**apekdysei**) of the body of the flesh' has been mentioned in v. 11, and 'the flesh' could be understood as the object here, although it is not specifically mentioned. Many of the early scholars certainly interpreted the passage this way. For example, Novatian (*On the Trinity*, 16) says, 'having put off the flesh, he disgraced the powers (*exutus carnem, potestates dehonestavit*)', and similar interpretations are given by Hilary, Ambrose and Augustine. On the other hand, it can be argued that the easier option is to take 'the rulers and authorities' as the object of the participle, since they are already the object of the main verb in the sentence. Fallen humanity

was in subjection to 'the rulers and authorities', and Christ by his incarnation took on the 'body of the flesh' which was under their domination. By his death he conquered them and, in divesting himself of the flesh, also divested himself, and all mankind, of their domination. Perhaps both 'the flesh' and 'the rulers and authorities' are the object of the verb **apek-dûsamenos**.

There is, however, a third option, which is to assume that the object is 'clothes'. It may seem a rather crude and literal interpretation, but it contains a remarkable paradox. When Christ was crucified he was naked, a humiliating and disgraceful experience in itself, particularly for a Jew. This disgrace, however, rebounded upon 'the rulers and authorities' when he rose triumphant from the dead. In other words, the one who had been stripped and humiliated was the one who humiliated the powers that had dominated the world before his triumph. The strongest argument for this interpretation is that grammatically speaking, the lack of an object is no problem, since **apekdûsamenos** on its own, i.e. without an object, like the commoner single prefix forms of this verb, **apodûsamenos** and **ekdûsamenos**, would normally mean 'having undressed', i.e. 'naked'. I prefer to believe that all three interpretations are valid, since either of the first two could be regarded as a *hiddush*, in other words, a hidden meaning contained within the literal text.

'Openly', **en parrhêsiâi**, literally 'in (or 'with') free speech', since to speak freely is, by extension, to be seen to act boldly in public. See my notes on Heb. 3.6 in *Reading Through Hebrews*.

'Made an example of', **edeigmatisen**, literally, 'made a show of', hence 'put to shame'. Just as Christ was made a shameful spectacle by his crucifixion, so his enemies have suffered the same fate. Heb. 6.6 interestingly also associates crucifixion with 'making a show of' in a passage which refers to apostates vainly trying to be reinstated since they are 'crucifying for themselves anew the son of God and *making a spectacle of* him (**paradeigmatizontas**)'.

'Triumphed over them on it' may strike us a grotesque image of Christ riding on his cross at the head of a triumphal procession followed by the captive 'rulers and authorities'. Paul, however, seems occasionally to use metaphors without being conscious of their visual impact, and here he probably intended merely to say that it was the cross which enabled Christ to triumph over the powers of this world. In other words, it probably means 'triumphed over them *by* it'. **En autôi**, 'on it', can also mean 'by *him*', i.e. Christ, but this would only be possible if God, not Christ, were the subject of this sentence. The Vulgate has *in semet ipso*, 'in himself', but this seems to have been due to a variation found in the early Latin versions of this passage, perhaps based on the third interpretation I have outlined above. In other words, having been humiliated, he brought humiliation on them *by his own humiliation*.

16 So let no one judge you in the matter of food and drink, or in respect of a feast, a new moon or sabbaths. 17 These are a shadow of what was to come, but the substance belongs to Christ. 18 Let no one make judgment against you because he delights in fasting and angel worship, things which he has seen in some initiation, vainly puffed up by his fleshly mind 19 and not keeping hold of the Head from which the whole body, being supplied and put together through its joints and ligaments, grows as God intends.

[16] The reference here is clearly to some form of Judaism and sums up the previous argument. The verse echoes part of Ezek. 45.17 (AV), '. . . meat offerings, and drink offerings, in the feasts, and in the new moons, and in the sabbaths'. Lightfoot has pointed out that many of the features referred to in this and verses 18 and 23 were characteristic of the strict Jewish sect of the Essenes, and draws attention to Josephus (*Jewish War*, II,

119–142). Josephus tells us that on the sabbath they would not light a fire, move any vessel or even defecate. They avoided marriage, and those who did marry had to avoid intercourse once a child was conceived. They drank no wine and ate no animal food. They did not believe in the resurrection of the body but rather the immortality of the soul, which was released on death from the corruption of the material world. On being admitted to full membership of their sect they had to swear an oath that they would guard carefully their sacred scriptures and not reveal the names of the angels.

'In respect', **en merei**, literally, 'in part', a phrase denoting 'in the category', 'in the matter'.

[17] 'Shadow', **skiâ**, is contrasted with 'substance', literally, 'body', **sôma**.

'Of what was to come', **tôn mellontôn**.

This verse is remarkably similar to Heb. 10.1, 'For the Law holds a *shadow* (**skiân**) *of the good things to come* (**tôn mellontôn agathôn**), not the actual form of reality.' It also echoes Heb. 8.4–5, which says of the Temple high priests, 'There are those who offer gifts according to the Law, who serve with a picture and a *shadow* (**skiâi**) of the heavenly place.' The use of the word **sôma**, 'body', is intriguing, since in the context of Colossians and Ephesians we are bound to think of its use to refer to the church, and because we are also led to think of the incarnation. As one of the earliest heresies to emerge in the infant church was Docetism, the belief that the physical body of Christ was some sort of illusion, either because God could not take on flesh or because matter was regarded as evil, could Paul be deliberately drawing attention to the reality of the incarnation?

[18] 'Make judgment against', **katabrabeuetô**, from the noun **brabeus**, 'umpire'.

'Because he delights in', **thelôn en**, literally, 'willing in', a literal translation found in the Septuagint of a Hebrew expression. The AV 'voluntary' does not express this idiom.

'Fasting', **tapeinophrosynêi**, literally, 'humble thinking', a secondary meaning of this noun which normally denotes 'modesty' or 'humility', as in 3.12 and Eph. 4.2. See the notes on the former. The connection between humility and fasting can be seen in such early Christian works as The Shepherd of Hermas (*Vision* 3, 10.6), 'Every request needs *humility* (**tapeinophrosynês**). So fast, and you will receive what you ask from the Lord.'

'Angel worship', **thrêskeiâi tôn angelôn**, need not be taken too literally. It may refer to the superstitious practices of popular Judaism, where the aid of particular angels was invoked in the problems of everyday life, or it could refer either to some heretical cult which combined Judaism with pagan rituals, or to the Essenes with their secret knowledge of the names of angels. We associate the Essenes with Palestine, but it is possible that they or related sects could also be found in the province of Asia.

'Things which he has seen in some initiation', **ha heorâken embateuôn**, is probably the most obscure clause in the letter. It is not helped by the fact that the text is also suspect, some manuscripts adding 'not' to the verb 'has seen'. Commentators have been tempted to emend the passage radically, but this urge to emend merely illustrates their frustration. The core of the problem is the participle **embateuôn.** Here is a list of suggested interpretations:

1. entering into,
2. taking his stand on,
3. investigating,
4. coming into possession of (e.g. promised land),
5. being initiated into (e.g. mysteries),
6. frequenting, haunting.

The weakest of these is the third interpretation, 'investigating', because it conveys little and, more seriously, because it is not found in this sense. The second interpretation, 'taking his stand on', would have been plausible, but it too, unfortunately, is not one of the meanings of **embateuôn**. Although the fourth, 'coming into possession of', is a well-attested meaning, it is difficult to see the relevance here. Most of the early readers of this letter would have followed the first interpretation, 'entering into things he has seen', but would have been puzzled by its relevance in this context. Hence it is likely that they inserted the negative, because 'entering into matters which he has *not* seen' makes good sense, and is the one favoured by the AV, 'intruding into those things which he hath not seen'. The Vulg. *quae non vidit ambulans frustra* also contains the inserted negative, but, leaving aside the question whether *frustra*, 'in vain', should go with *ambulans*, *ambulans*, 'walking about', does come close to one of the possible meanings for **embateuôn**, 'frequent, haunt'. If we assume that there can be no negative, since the best manuscripts do not contain it, we are left with the last two interpretations: 'things which he has seen while being initiated' and 'things which he has seen as he walks around'. I have favoured the former, because there are good examples in inscriptions of this meaning, but am not entirely convinced that this is the right interpretation.

'Vainly puffed up', **eikêi phûsioumenos**, is an interesting expression. This verb is used six times in I Corinthians and nowhere else in the NT except here. The metaphor reminds one of the frog who puffs himself up until he bursts, and seems to denote arrogance or pride. Coincidentally, Strabo (*Geography*, XIII, c. 630) speaks of an underground chamber at Hierapolis, called the Plutonium, where the resident eunuch priests demonstrated their powers of immunity by taking a deep breath secretly before subjecting themselves to its poisonous atmosphere. By holding their breath, i.e. by being 'puffed up', they could survive an experience which was fatal for animals or the uninitiated. Could this be a topical and humorous reference to a pagan shrine which would have been familiar to his audience? Strabo's description of them almost suffocating as they held their breath is strangely appropriate.

'By his fleshly mind', literally, 'by the mind of his flesh', i.e.

'thinking in a non-spiritual or materialistic way'. For a fuller discussion of the significance of 'flesh', **sarx**, and 'spirit', **pneuma**, see the notes on Gal. 5.17 in *Reading Through Galatians*.


[19] This verse clearly corresponds to the longer version in Eph. 4.16. They both introduce as their theme the head (i.e. Christ), followed by 'from which the whole body . . .', and there are several terms which appear in both passages, such as **haphê**, 'a joint'; **symbibazomenon**, 'being put together'; **auxêsis**, 'an increase'; and here the verb **epichorêgoumenon**, 'being supplied' takes the place of the noun **epichorêgiâ**, 'a supply' in Ephesians. The differences are discussed in the notes on Eph. 4.16.

'From which', **ex hou**, uses a masculine relative pronoun, although the noun to which it refers, **kephalên**, 'head', is feminine. Clearly Paul is referring to Christ.

'Being supplied . . . through', **epichorêgoumenon . . . dia**, rather than 'furnished . . . by'. The joints and ligaments are the channels *through which* Christ the head supplies what the rest of the body needs; they are not *what* he supplies.

'Grows as God intends', **auxei tên auxêsin tou Theou**, literally, 'increases the increase of God'.


20 If you have escaped by death with Christ from the elemental powers of the world, why do you subject yourselves to ordinances as though your life is in the world, 21 'don't handle, don't taste, don't touch', 22 all things which are destined to be destroyed in being used, according to the commandments and teachings of human beings, 23 and which carry a reputation for wisdom with devotion to religious practices, fasting and severity towards the body, but which are worthless in dealing with sensual indulgence?

[20] 'Escaped by death from', literally, 'died from'. This is different from the usual Pauline expression 'dying to', as in Gal. 2.19, 'I have died to the Law', **nomôi apethanon**, because it is placing emphasis on escape and separation from the domination of the elemental powers.

For 'the elemental powers of the world', **tôn stoicheiôn tou kosmou,** see the notes on v. 8.

'Subject yourselves to ordinances', **dogmatizesthe.**

'As though your life is in the world', **hôs zôntes en kosmôi,** literally, 'as living in the world', refers to eternal, spiritual life (**zôê**) which comes from outside this world; physical, biological life (**bios**) is in this world. As 3.3 says, 'your life has been hidden with Christ in God'. The Christian is no longer under the control of the 'rulers and authorities' of this world.


[21] This verse roughly summarizes the dietary and purificatory rules of the Mosaic Law, but would also apply to the stricter ordinances of the Essenes.


[22] 'Destined to be destroyed in being used', **eis phthorân têi apochrêsei,** literally, 'for destruction by use', simply refers to the fact that the commandments of the Law referred to above are concerned with material things, such as food and clothes, which are used up or wear away, not about eternal things. As Theodoret crudely puts it, 'all is changed into excrement'.

'Commandments and teachings of human beings', **ta entalmata kai didaskaliâs tôn anthrôpôn** most probably comes from Isa. 29.13 (Sept.), 'In vain do they worship me , teaching the *commandments and teachings of men* (**entalmata anthrôpôn kai didaskaliâs**).' This makes it even clearer that Paul is referring to the Mosaic Law and its commandments. See also the note on 'human tradition' in v. 8.


[23] This is a notoriously difficult verse, although I would not go as far as Moule, who says, 'This verse is by common consent

regarded as hopelessly obscure – either owing to corruption or because we have lost the clue.'

'And which carry a reputation for wisdom', **hatina estin logon men echonta sophiâs**, literally, 'which are having on the one hand a word of wisdom'. The word translated as 'reputation' is **logon**, which is often contrasted in Greek literature with **ergon**, 'deed' or 'reality'. For example, the English sentence 'The Athenians pretended to make peace but in fact were preparing for war' would come out in Greek as '*In pretence, on the one hand* (**logôi men**) the Athenians made peace, *in reality, on the other hand* (**ergôi de**) they were preparing for war.' So Paul apparently is saying that the commandments and their associated rituals only *seem* to be wise. The AV 'have a shew of wisdom' supports this interpretation. The Vulg. *rationem habentia sapientiae* seems to take **logon** in the sense of 'system', 'theory', and makes a similar point, i.e. they are theoretically wise but in fact foolish. **Logos** can also mean 'statement', 'formula' or 'expression', and any of these meanings would give us a similar interpretation.

'Devotion to religious practices', **ethelothrêskiâi**, a word found nowhere else. 'Voluntary worship' is the obvious meaning, if we follow the analogy with other compounds prefixed by **ethelo-**, but [e]**thelôn** in v. 18, 'delighting in', probably is the meaning here. The Vulg. *superstitione* supports this interpretation.

'Worthless in dealing with sensual indulgence', **ouk en tîmêi tini pros plêsmonên tês sarkos**, literally, 'not in any value in regard to the filling up of the flesh'. Note that Paul omits the particle **de**, 'on the other hand', 'but', which would normally be used to balance the previous **men**, 'on the one hand'. **Tîmê** is commonly translated as 'honour', but frequently means 'price' or 'value'. **Plêsmonê** occurs nowhere else in the NT, but in other works denotes 'surfeit', especially that associated with food. The meaning seems to be that all the religious practices referred to above with their occasional austerities are useless in dealing with engrained habits of indulgence in bodily pleasures. It is no good fasting on one day, if you gorge yourself on other days. Some commentators try to extract from this phrase the meaning 'treating the flesh (or body) with no respect in regard to satisfying its desires', but it is difficult see how **en tîmêi** can govern either **sarkos**, 'flesh', since **sarkos** is dependent on **plêsmonên**, or **sôma**, 'body', which is not even in the same clause. In addition, this interpretation is hardly relevant in the context. Another suggestion is 'which are of no value, but only tend to sensual indulgence', but such an interpretation is also inappropriate, and, by introducing 'but only', stretches the syntax too far.

# Chapter 3

1 So if you were raised together with Christ, seek the things above, where Christ is seated on the right hand of God. 2 Keep your minds on things above, not things on earth. 3 For you died and your life has been hidden with Christ in God. 4 When Christ, your life, is revealed, then you, too, will be revealed with him in glory.

[1] 'You were raised together', **synêgerthête**, refers back to 2.12.

'Seek the things above', **ta anô zêteite,** is not a call to despise the material world. 'The things above' are the eternal things, but they also represent the future kingdom of Christ. Christians have died to this world and been raised with Christ to the new life which is with Christ in heaven. Since many pagan philosophers treated the world of matter as inferior, one can see how easy it would be for the early convert to misunderstand such statements as 'seek the things above', and assume that Paul is preaching a gospel of detachment from the world based on a philosophy which believed that the pure spirit was polluted by contact with material things. Docetism, Gnosticism and its off-shoot, Manichaeism, are such philosophies.

[2] 'Keep your minds on things above', **ta anô phroneite**, i.e 'think the things above'.

[3] 'Hidden', not just out of sight, but stored away safely. The new life may not be obvious now, but it will be.

[4] Just as the new life will be revealed, so the glory which the Christian will inherit is hidden at present. It is the 'hope of glory' of 1.27.

5 So put to death your earthly members [in regard to] fornication, filthiness, passion, wicked desire and the excess of idolatry. 6 Because of these things, God's anger is visited on the children of disobedience. 7 These were [the vices] in which you, too, once walked when your life was bound up with them.

[5] Because you have died with Christ you must treat your body as dead to your former sins. 'Put to death', **nekrôsate**, is a strong expression, but it is not the same as 'mortify', which carries the sense of inflicting some pain on one's body. It is used figuratively – 'treat as though it were a corpse'.

'Your earthly members', **ta melê ta epi tês gês**, literally, 'the limbs on the earth', is a strange expression. Lightfoot may be right in assuming this is a synonym for 'the old man', **ton palaion anthrôpon,** of v. 9. It could also mean simply 'your physical body', i.e. 'the body which you inhabit while you are on the earth'. Compare I Cor. 15.47, 'The first man is of the earth, made of dust; the second man is from heaven.'

Some of the vices referred to here are found in Eph. 5.3, 'fornication . . . filthiness . . . excess', and in Eph. 4.19, 'filthiness . . . excess'.

'Filthiness', or 'impurity', **akatharsiâ**, as I point out in the notes on Gal. 5.19 in *Reading Through Galatians*, refers to any immoral sexual activity not covered by 'fornication', **porneiâ**. There is no justification for translating **akatharsiâ** as 'covetousness'.

'Passion, wicked desire', **pathos epithûmiân kakên,** should probably be taken together, as in I Thess. 4.5, which also refers to sexual desire, 'not *in the passion of desire* (en pathei epithûmiâs), like the Gentiles, in fact, who do not know God'.

'The excess of idolatry', tên pleonexiân hêtis estin eidôlolatriâ, literally, 'excess, which is idolatry'. This expression has been frequently misunderstood. Firstly, pleonexiân means 'trying to have more than one should', and originally referred to greediness or ambition, as it does in I Thess. 2.5. But it also denotes any activity which could be described as 'going over the top', i.e. exceeding the limit. Secondly, there is no reason to translate this phrase as 'excess (or 'covetousness'), which is *a form of* idolatry'. It is not to be taken metaphorically, as some translators assume, but as a reference to the actual sin of idolatry, 'worship of idols', as in I Corinthians (5.10, 11; 6.9; 10.7). I Cor. 10.7 is particularly relevant: 'and don't be idolaters, as some of them were, as it is written, " the people sat down to eat and drink and stood up to play".' It is impossible to point to a single case in the NT of either 'idolater' or 'idolatry' being used unambiguously in a metaphorical sense. The parallel passage in Ephesians (5.5) has pleonektês ho estin eidôlolatrês, 'who indulges to excess, that is, an idolater', which makes this point much more clearly.

[6] 'God's anger' is a recurrent theme in Paul's letters, particularly Romans. It is virtually a synonym for 'judgment' or 'condemnation'; hence the expression 'the day of anger', i.e. 'the day of final judgment', in Rom. 2.5 and Rev. 6.17.

The phrase 'children (sons) of disobedience' occurs also in Eph. 2.2 and 5.6. It is a translation of a Hebrew expression meaning 'disobedient people'. Some manuscripts omit the whole phrase 'on the children of disobedience' and it may be that it was introduced here to conform with Eph. 5.6, the parallel passage. The opposite expression is found in 1 Peter 1.14, 'children of obedience'.

[7] 'Your life was bound up with them', ezête en toutois,

literally, 'you lived in them'. There is a paradox here; this was not true 'life', since it led to death.

8  But now you, too, [must] put aside all the [following]: bad temper, anger, malice, and, from your mouths, abuse and shameful talk. 9 Do not lie to one another, since you have put off the old man along with his deeds, 10 and have put on the new [man] who is being renewed into knowledge according to the image of the one who formed him, 11 where one is not Greek or Jew, [where] circumcision or uncircumcision [do not count], [where one is not] a barbarian, Scythian, slave or free, but [where] Christ is all in all.

[8] 'You, too', **kai hûmeis**, seems odd. It looks as though 'you' is being contrasted with someone else, but no one else has been mentioned. Does Paul mean 'as well as your Jewish Christian brethren'? It is more likely that 'you, too' is a rhetorical repetition, for the sake of emphasis, of 'you, too' in v. 7. Note also the awkward phrase 'from your mouths', which in the original is added, almost like an after-thought, at the end of the sentence. It is difficult to see how it could go with 'put aside' in respect of all the vices in this verse. I have assumed it goes with the last two, but it may be that Paul saw all the vices mentioned as being manifested in what one said as much as in what one did.

The vices mentioned in this verse are repeated in Eph. 4.31, without 'shameful talk', but with the addition of 'bitterness' and 'shouting'. The Ephesians passage is more carefully crafted. Typically, the Colossians passage is more condensed.

'Bad temper', **orgên**; 'anger', **thûmon**; 'malice', **kakiân**; 'abuse', **blasphêmiân**. See the notes on Eph. 4.31 for these four vices.

'Shameful talk', **aischrologiân**, does not occur anywhere else in the NT. It is the term used in Aristotle (*Nicomachean Ethics*,

1128a, 23) to describe the obscene humour of the Old Comedy in Athens. Incidentally, it is intriguing that I have had occasion to quote this particular work of Aristotle seven times while writing this guide in order to define terms used in these letters. Had Paul been reading the book during his captivity?

[9] 'Put off', **apekdûsamenoi**; see note on 2.15.

'The old man', **ton palaion anthrôpon**, a term found in Rom. 6.6, recalls Eph. 4.22. Again the Colossians passage is more condensed; 'along with his deeds' is represented in the Ephesians version by 'of your former life, who perishes in the pursuit of his deceitful desires'.

[10] 'The new [man]', **ton neon**, corresponds to the 'new man', **kainon anthrôpon**, of Eph. 4.24, 'who was created in accordance with God in the righteousness and holiness of truth'. **Neon** is probably used here for stylistic reasons, since the root **kain-** occurs in the participle 'being renewed', **anakainoumenon**. The differences between the two versions are instructive. Firstly, the emphasis here is on the continuous process of renewal by conforming with the divine pattern, where the Ephesians parallel is more static. Secondly, renewal in Colossians is characterized by an increase in knowledge (**epignôsin**), which is not mentioned in Ephesians. Who is the 'new man'? Is it Christ himself, or is it the ideal person that the Christian becomes? The use of the word 'image', **eikona**, recalling 1.15, would indicate that Christ is *the pattern* for this new man, not the man himself. Furthermore, Christ can hardly be described as 'being renewed into knowledge', and the notion that God 'formed', **ktisantos**, i.e. 'created', him seems inappropriate, if God, indeed, is 'the one who formed'. Chrysostom, for instance, thought 'the one who formed' was Christ. The Ephesians version also seems to point towards the idea that the 'new man' refers to the perfected Christian. At the same time, we can detect in Paul's thinking two different concepts of the 'new man', the first being the person that the Christian is meant

to become, *a* new Adam, an image of perfection created by God, as in Eph. 2.15, and the second being Christ himself, *the* new Adam, the 'perfect man', **andra teleion**, of Eph. 4.13 and the eternal image of God referred to in 1.15. As 'we shall carry the image of the heavenly [man]' (I Cor. 15.49), the Christian is a 'new man', after the pattern of the 'new man' Christ. The same ambivalence can be seen in the metaphor of the church as the body of Christ: the Christian is in Christ, being part of his body, yet at the same time is separate from him, since Christ is the head of the body, and the Christian merely a part of the rest of the body.

[11] This verse is very close to Gal. 3.28, 'In him one is not Jew or Greek, one is not slave or freeman, one is not male or female, for you are all one in Christ Jesus.' In both passages we have the word **eni**, which is an abbreviation for **enesti**, meaning 'is included', 'is present', 'is possible', taking the place of the normal word **esti**, 'is'. Paul is not saying that Greek, i.e. Gentile, and Jew do not exist, but that as far as their status as Christians goes, they are equal; as the NEB puts it, 'There is no question here of Greek and Jew.' On this subject see my notes in *Reading Through Galatians*.

'Where', i.e. in Christ, in the church.

'Scythian', being a stereotype for those who spoke a barbaric form of Greek, represents a status half way between the 'barbarian', who is the non-Greek speaker, and the native Greek speaker. There is no need to regard the 'Scythian' as the lowest form of barbarian, as Lightfoot suggests. Scythians were familiar in the eastern parts of the Mediterranean, and in classical Athens acted as policemen.

'All in all', **panta kai en pâsin**, literally, 'all [things] and in all', i.e. Christ is all that counts and this is so in every aspect of life. It is impossible to know whether **pâsin** is neuter or masculine, 'in all *things*' or 'in all *people*'. A similar problem occurs in Eph. 4.6. I have assumed here that it is neuter like **panta**.

12 So, as chosen and loved saints of God, put on the heart of compassion, kindness, modesty, gentleness and patience, 13 being tolerant towards one another and forgiving each other, if anyone of you has any reason to blame someone else; just as the Lord forgave you, so you [must] also [forgive]. 14 And, above all these, [put on] love, which is the bond of perfection. 15 And let the peace of Christ be the guiding principle in your hearts, since it is for this that you were called in one body, and be thankful.

[12] 'Put on' is an odd word to use here; 'putting on' the 'new man', as one 'puts on' a coat, is a reasonable metaphor, but 'putting on' virtues seems inappropriate. Paul, however, continues with the same metaphor because he is defining the characteristics of the 'new man'.

'Heart of compassion', **splangchna oiktirmou**, literally, 'inner parts of pity'. **Splangchna** is a metaphor for the seat of the emotions. In Phil. 2.1 we have **splangchna kai oiktirmoi**, AV, 'bowels and mercies', which means the same.

'Kindness', **chrêstotêta**, in classical writers often denotes soft-heartedness or kind naivety. It does not have this derogatory sense in the NT.

'Modesty', or 'humility', **tapeinophrosynên**, is a particularly Christian virtue. Where it occurs in non-Christian writers, such as Josephus and Epictetus, it generally is 'meanness of spirit'. Chrysostom defines it as the state 'when someone who is important humbles himself', and 'when someone, knowing he has achieved something great, does not imagine great things about himself'. Pretending to have done nothing great, when you know you actually have, is false modesty.

'Gentleness', **prâytêta**, the opposite of irritability and bad temper, reacting mildly in aggressive situations. There is an adjectival form, **prâÿs**, which occurs in the Sermon on the Mount (Matt. 5.5), 'Blessed are the *meek* (**prâeis**)'. More striking is Matt.11.29, which quotes Jesus as saying, 'I am *meek* (**prâÿs**) and *humble* (**tapeinos**) in heart.' The association of the two qualities is clearly part of early moral teaching based on the words of Jesus.

'Patience', **makrothûmiân**, translated in 1.11 as 'long-suffering'. See the note on that verse. 'Modesty, gentleness and patience' occur together also in Eph. 4.2.

[13] 'Being tolerant', **anechomenoi**, 'putting up with', 'bearing with', is used in Eph. 4.2.

'Forgiving', **charizomenoi**, as in Eph. 4.32. Eph. 4.2 and 32 combined cover most of the content of verses 12 and 13 in this passage. See note on 2.13 regarding the verb **charizomai**.

[14] 'Bond of perfection', **syndesmos tês teleiotêtos**, a familiar metaphor in classical works. For example, Aristotle (*Nicomachean Ethics*, 1162a, 25) describes children as a **syndesmos** in a marriage: 'for those without children split up more quickly.' So, following this analogy, love holds the church together; it is the bond of union which demonstrates her perfection. The thought, expressed differently, is also found in Rom. 13.10, 'love is the *fulfilment* (**plêrôma**) of the Law'. See also Eph. 4.3, 'bond of peace'. In 2.19 we have the plural of **syndesmos** used to denote 'ligaments'. For the significance of the prefix **syn-** see the notes on 2.12; Eph. 2.6; 3.6 and 4.16.

[15] 'Of Christ' is a better reading than the AV's 'of God'.

'Be the guiding principle', **brabeuetô**, literally, 'let it be the umpire'. See the note on 2.18.

'For this', **eis hên**, refers to 'love', the whole purpose of being in Christ.

'Thankful', **eucharistoi**, a word used nowhere else in the NT. It can mean 'gracious, agreeable', but 'thankful' or 'grateful' is the likely meaning here, as it seems to be represented in Eph.

5.4 by the noun **eucharistiâ**, which must mean 'giving of thanks'.

16 Let the word of Christ live amongst you in its richness, teaching and counselling each other in every wise way, singing psalms, hymns and spiritual songs with gratefulness in your hearts to God. 17 And, whatever you do, in word or deed, [do] everything in the name of the Lord Jesus, thanking God the Father through him.

[16–17] These verses are echoed in Eph. 5.19–20.

'In its richness', **plousiôs**, literally, 'richly'.

'In every wise way', **en pâsêi sophiâi**, literally, 'in all wisdom'.

Scholars argue about these terms, but it is likely that the 'psalms' refer to the OT psalms, most probably in their Septuagint form; 'hymns' are songs which praise God, and therefore 'spiritual songs' must cover the rest of their repertoire.

'With gratefulness', NEB 'thankfully', **en chariti**, literally, 'in grace'. I have discussed **charis** in my notes on Gal. 1.3 and Heb. 12.28 in this series of guides. Since it appears that the phrase refers to a required response on the part of his audience, 'with gratefulness' is more appropriate than the more usual 'with (God's) grace', and fits in with the participle 'thanking', **eucharistountes** and the adjective 'thankful', **eucharistoi** of v. 15. 'With grace (i.e. charm) on your part' is an unlikely interpretation favoured by some commentators.

18 You wives, give way to your husbands, as would be right in the Lord. 19 You husbands, love your wives and do not be irritable with them. 20 You children, obey your parents in everything, for this is just what

pleases the Lord. 21 You fathers, do not provoke your children, in case they lose confidence.

[18] In Ephesians (5.22-24) the submission of wives to their husbands, which here is simply referred to in passing, is developed into a complex and subtle theological statement.

'As would be right in the Lord', **hôs anêken en Kûriôi**, uses the imperfect tense. Abbott suggests that it expresses an obligation which existed previously; it was right and still is right. But is Paul saying that wives should give way to their husbands because it is the Christian way, or that they should submit to them as though to Christ himself, in other words 'as is right to do *in the case of* the Lord'? If the latter, the imperfect tense can be taken in a conditional sense, 'as would be right *if the Lord were their husband*'. The Ephesians version, 'as though to the Lord', clearly supports the second interpretation.

[19] The implications of this brief sentence concerning the duties of husbands are brought out in a complex essay in Eph. 5.25-33.

'Be irritable with', i.e. 'get exasperated at', **pikrainesthe**, the only time this metaphorical usage is found in the NT. The verb **pikrainô** also occurs in Revelation but only in its literal sense, 'to make something taste bitter'.

[20] Again Ephesians (6.1-3) makes more of this simple command.

'Just what pleases the Lord', literally, 'well-pleasing in the Lord'.

[21] The Ephesians version (6.4) makes a clearer reference to discipline and education.

'Provoke', or 'irritate', **erethizete**, where Ephesians has 'make angry', **parorgizete**, which has the same meaning.

22 You slaves, obey your earthly masters in all matters, not with a show of service, like those who aim to
please human beings, but in the simplicity of your
heart and in the fear of the Lord. 23 Whatever you do,
do it from your soul as though you are working for the
Lord, not human beings, 24 knowing that you will
receive your reward, your inheritance from the Lord.
Serve the Master, Christ; 25 for the wrongdoer will get
his wrong back, and there is no partiality.

[22–25] The equivalent passage in Ephesians is 6.5–8.
Anyone who criticizes Paul for not attacking the institution of
slavery can have little conception of the consequences of such
an action in the first century AD. The Christian church did
gradually change the perception of people regarding slavery,
but it would have been foolhardy at this stage to challenge
openly a practice which underpinned the whole of ancient
civilization. Slave revolts were put down with extreme rigour
by the authorities, and preaching against slavery would have
been treated as a political act encouraging slaves to revolt.

[22] 'Your earthly masters', **tois kata sarka kûriois**, literally,
'the masters according to the flesh'.
   'Show of service', **ophthalmodouliâi**, literally, 'eye-service',
only found here and in Eph. 6.6.
   'Those who aim to please human beings', **anthrôpareskoi**,
literally, 'men-pleasers', another word used in Eph. 6.6, and
nowhere else in the NT, although it occurs in the Septuagint.
   'Simplicity', **haplotêti**, i.e. 'singleness', rather than 'sincerity'. Wisdom 1.1 uses the same phrase in this sense.

[23] The translation here has expanded the abbreviated expression 'whatever you do, work from the soul'.
   'From your soul', **ek psûchês**, where we might have expected
'from your heart', **ek kardiâs**. In fact, they are synonyms;

compare Mark 12.30, 'You shall love the Lord your God *with
all your heart* (**ex holês tês kardiâs sou**), and *with all your soul*
(**ex holês tês psûchês sou**).'

[24] 'Your reward, your inheritance', literally, 'the reward of
the inheritance'.

'Serve', **douleuete**, Vulg. *servite*, must be imperative, not
indicative, 'you are serving', since the other second-person
present-tense verbs, 'obey' and 'work', are clearly imperatives.
(A note for those who are not sure what point I am making: in
Greek the second person plural of the present tense can also be
a command or imperative, unlike Latin, which distinguishes
between the two, e.g. *servitis*, 'you serve, you are serving',
*servite*, 'serve'.)

'Master', **kûriôi**, which, of course, also means 'Lord'. The
title 'Lord Jesus', however, would be unusual, and translating
it so would obscure the point Paul is making, i.e. that slaves
and masters alike have a Master in heaven, a point he makes
explicit in 4.1 and Eph. 6.9.

[25] The emphasis here is on the punishment for wrong-
doing; in Eph. 6.8 it is on the reward for good deeds.

'Partiality', **prosôpolêmpsiâ**, the abstract noun from **pro-
sôpon lambanô**, literally, 'I take (i.e. accept) the face', occurs
also in Rom. 2.11 and Eph. 6.9. See my note on Gal. 2.6 in
*Reading Through Galatians*. With 'there is no partiality' we
must understand the phrase 'with God', as is made explicit in
Ephesians. We can also deduce from that passage that it refers
to God treating slave and master as equals when it comes to
judgment; Paul is not advocating the adoption of an egalitarian
stance in the matter of slavery or in any other social relationship.

# Chapter 4

1 You masters, treat your slaves rightly and fairly, knowing that you, too, have a Master in heaven. 2 Pray regularly, staying awake to do so, and give thanks, 3 praying at the same time also for us that God may open up for us a door for the gospel to speak the secret truth of Christ, because of which I am in prison, 4 so that I may explain it in the way that I should speak.

[1] 'Treat . . . rightly and fairly', **to dikaion kai tên isotêta . . . parechesthe**, literally, 'offer justice and fairness'. Although the core meaning of the noun **isotês** is 'equality', the meaning 'fair dealing' is common and more appropriate here. The Ephesians version (6.9) of this verse makes it clear that it is only God who treats slaves and masters as equals.

[2] Eph 6.18 is the parallel, and fuller, version of this verse.

'Pray regularly', **têi proseuchêi proskartereite**, literally, 'persist in prayer'.

'Staying awake to do so', **grêgorountes en autêi**, literally, 'being awake in it'. The NEB 'with mind awake' gives this phrase a metaphorical bias which the original does not have. Lightfoot also believes that it is to be taken as a metaphor. But the Ephesians version, 'keeping watch *for this purpose* (**eis auto**)', removes any ambiguity. This command of Paul is as

literal as the command of Jesus when he found his disciples had
fallen asleep at Gethsemane, 'Watch and pray', **grêgoreite kai
proseuchesthe** (Matt. 26.41). The Ephesians version also adds
that the prayer should be 'for all the saints', not just for oneself,
but does not include any specific mention of thanksgiving.

'And give thanks', **en eucharistiâi**, literally, 'in thanksgiving'.

[3, 4] Eph. 6.19, 20 is the parallel version of this passage.

Compare 'open up for us a door for the gospel' with the
Ephesians 'be given the words when I open my mouth'. The
word I translate as 'gospel' is **logou**, i.e. 'the word of truth' of
1.5, but it could also mean 'speech'. Paul may mean simply 'the
door of speech', i.e. 'my mouth'. The AV 'a door of utterance'
means an opportunity to preach. The Vulg. *ostium sermonis*
could cover both interpretations, and there is no reason why
we have to reject one in favour of the other. The metaphorical
use of 'door', **thyrâ**, is well-established in the NT: for example,
John 10.7, 'I am the door of the sheep', i.e. the way by which
they can come into the fold, and Acts 14.27, 'he had opened the
door of faith to the Gentiles'

'The secret truth of Christ', **to mystêrion tou Christou**,
becomes 'the secret [truth] of *the gospel* (**tou euangeliou**)' in
Ephesians.

'In the way that I should speak', **hôs dei me lalêsai**, the same
phrase which is found in Ephesians, rather than 'since I have to
speak'. The NEB 'as it is my duty to do' seems to favour the
latter.

5 Behave sensibly in your relations with those outside
[the faith], not squandering your time. 6 [Let] your
conversation at all times [be] beneficial and shrewd,
and know how you should respond to each individual.
7 Tychicus, our dear brother and faithful servant and
fellow-slave in the Lord, will let you know how
everything stands with me. 8 I have sent him to you for

this very purpose, so that you may know about our situation and so that he can boost your morale, 9 together with Onesimus, our faithful and dear brother, who is one of you; they will let you know everything happening here.

[5] 'Behave sensibly', **en sophiâi peripateite**, literally, 'walk in wisdom'.

'Those outside', **tous exô**, a synonym for 'those who are distant' (Eph. 2.17). This term was originally applied by Jews to Gentiles outside the Law, but is used by Paul in I Cor. 5.12, 13 to refer to non-Christians. I Thess. 4.12 expresses the same thought: 'so that you may live respectable lives *in the sight of outsiders* (**pros tous exô**)'. See also the note on 'near' in Eph. 2.13.

'Not squandering your time', **ton kairon exagorazomenoi**, literally, 'buying up the opportunity'. This is an obscure expression, found also in Eph. 5.16, which has had many interpretations, such as 'gaining (or 'buying') time', and 'seizing the opportunity'. The Vulgate translates it as *tempus redimentes*, an obscure expression itself. In the context we would expect it to mean something like 'not wasting time', since the end of this world is approaching. 'Buying up' suggests the commercial colloquialism 'making a corner in the market', hence 'exploiting', 'making good use of'.

[6] 'Beneficial', **en chariti**, literally, 'in grace'. **Charis** can be 'grace', 'joy', 'charm', 'favour', 'gratitude' or, as here, 'boon', i.e. 'benefit'. See the notes on 3.16; Eph.1.6 and 4.29, and on Gal.1.3 in *Reading Through Galatians*. As this verse is clearly the parallel to Eph. 4.29, where I translate **charin** as 'benefit', 'beneficial' is the likely interpretation here.

'Shrewd', **halati êrtûmenos**, literally, 'prepared (or 'seasoned') with salt'. 'Salt' is a culinary reference probably referring to the use of salt to make food palatable. Hence, it means here the careful preparation of what you say, so that it is good to hear, just as carefully prepared food is good to eat. There is no reason for assuming that 'salt' is 'wit'; that is a Latin idiom. It is more likely to be a rabbinic idiom, where salt serves as an image of wise instruction. For instance, we have the saying 'the Torah is like salt'. Salt preserves food from corruption and so makes it wholesome.

[7] 'Tychicus', 'Lucky' or 'Fortunate', would have had the Latin name *Fortunatus*. Could this be the same person as the Fortunatus of I Cor. 16.17? We meet Tychicus again in Eph. 6.21. He seems to have been used a great deal by Paul to convey messages, and he would have known what was happening in Rome. As we know from Acts 20.4, he was a native of the province of Asia and would have been familiar with fellow Christians in such towns as Ephesus, Laodicaea and Colossae.

'Servant', **diâkonos**, or 'minister', soon became the title for an ordained officer in the church with special functions.

[8] This verse is exactly the same as Eph. 6.22. It is the sort of sentence that many letters might contain. 'That you may know about our situation' in some manuscripts is 'that *I* (or 'he') may know about *your* situation'. Hence the AV translates, 'that he might know your estate'.

'Boost your morale', literally, 'encourage your hearts'.

[9] 'Onesimus' is a fascinating figure. He was in all probability the same runaway slave whom Paul befriended and later persuaded to return to his master Philemon. 'Who is one of you' must mean that he came from Colossae.

10 Aristarchus, my fellow prisoner, sends you his regards, and Mark, Barnabas' cousin (you have received instructions regarding the latter; if he comes to you, make him welcome), 11 and Jesus, who is called

Justus, the only ones of the circumcision who are working with me for the kingdom of God, have been a comfort to me. 12 Epaphras, who is one of you, a slave of Christ Jesus, sends his regards. He is at all times striving on your behalf in his prayers so that you may stand perfect and complete in everything that God wills.

[10] 'Aristarchus', as we learn from Acts 19.29; 20.4; 27.2, was from Thessalonica in Macedonia, and must have been a Gentile. Whether he actually was in prison with Paul is difficult to know. The term used here is figurative, **synaichmalôtos**, i.e. 'fellow prisoner *of war*'. Does that mean 'conquered by Christ' or 'taken prisoner by our opponents'?

'Mark', the cousin of Barnabas, was Jewish. 'Cousin' is the more usual meaning of **anepsios**. It only came to mean 'nephew' in later Greek. He is mentioned several times in Acts and Paul knew him from his early missionary days in Cyprus, where he is introduced under his Hebrew name 'John'. He assisted Barnabas, Paul and Peter at different times. In I Peter 5.13 he is referred to as Peter's 'son'.

[11] 'Jesus', i.e. 'Joshua', a common Jewish name, has been given the similarly sounding Roman name, 'Justus'. The statement that he and Mark were the only Jewish Christians to be of comfort to Paul is significant. If Paul is in Rome, where there were many Jewish Christians, it may be evidence that several of these churches were tending to Judaize. I have argued in the introduction to *Reading Through Hebrews* that the letter to the Hebrews was probably addressed to these churches. Since the main theme of that letter is a warning against Judaizing, the fact that Paul was receiving so little help from Jewish Christians would support my hypothesis.

[12] 'Epaphras': see note on 1.7.

'Stand', i.e. most probably in the sense of being able to stand triumphant before the judgment seat of God, as we see from Rev. 6.17, 'For the great day of their anger (i.e. 'judgment') has come, and who can stand?', and Rev. 7.9, 'a great crowd ... standing before the throne ... clothed with white robes and with palm branches in their hands'.

'Perfect and complete', **teleioi kai peplêrophorêmenoi**. The latter is the only example of the use of the verb **plêrophoreô** in Colossians and Ephesians. **Plêroô**, which means much the same, occurs eight times. Consequently it is not surprising that some manuscripts have **peplêrômenoi**, from **plêroô**. Some commentators interpret **peplêrophorêmenoi** as 'fully assured' or 'convinced', but this is a rare usage, as I point out in my notes on the noun **plêrophoriâ** in 2.2. See also the notes on Eph. 1.23 regarding **plêroô**.

'In everything that God wills', **en panti thelêmati tou Theou**, literally, 'in every wish of God'; in other words, that you may be made as perfect as God wishes you to be, and that you may fulfil completely the tasks that God wants you to carry out.

13 For I am a witness for him that he takes great pains on behalf of you and those in Laodicaea and Hierapolis. 14 Luke, our dear doctor, sends you his regards and [so does] Demas. 15 Greet our brothers and sisters in Laodicaea together with Nymphas and the church in their house. 16 And when this letter is read to you, make sure that it is also read in the church of the Laodicaeans, and that you also read the letter from Laodicaea. 17 And say to Archippus, 'See that you fulfil the ministry which you have taken on in the Lord.' 18 Signing off in my own hand, Paul. Remember my chains. Grace be with you.

[13] 'He takes great pains', **echei polyn ponon**, literally, 'he has much toil'.

'Laodicaea and Hierapolis': see note on 2.1.

[14] There can be little doubt that this 'dear doctor' is the evangelist.

'Demas', most probably an abbreviation of 'Demetrius'. He is mentioned in II Tim.4.10 as having deserted Paul 'because he loved the present world'.


[15] Is it 'Nymphas', masculine, or 'Nympha', feminine? Is it 'his' or 'her' church? The second question is the easier to answer, and will also give us the answer to the first question. The best manuscripts generally have 'their', **autôn**, although a few have 'his', **autou**. 'His' seems to have crept in because it is odd to say 'Nymphas and *their* church', but Paul probably means 'Nymphas and his household and their church'. The reading 'her', **autês**, is even less likely than 'his', since there are few good manuscripts with this reading. It looks as though some scribe, seeing the name **Nymphan**, assumed it was feminine, although in Greek many nouns which are actually masculine have this characteristically feminine accusative ending. Furthermore, there is a grammatical argument against the person referred to here being female; the accusative ending -**an** would make the name 'Nymph*â*', a Doric form. This is impossible in the dialect of Greek Paul is using, since the correct form in that dialect is always 'Nymph*ê*'. Despite this, most modern translations, such as the NEB, Moffatt and the Jerusalem Bible, have a female 'Nympha' and 'her house'. 'Nymphas', as an abbreviation for 'Nymphodorus' is similar to other names we have already met in these letters. This type of abbreviated name is probably only found in certain areas; it certainly seems common in the province of Asia. Incidentally the Vulg. translation, *Nympham, et quae in domo eius est ecclesia*, throws no light on this issue, since it could apply to either gender.


[16] The obvious meaning of this verse is that Colossae and Laodicaea were meant to exchange the letters Paul had sent to each church. It is a perverse interpretation to take 'from

Laodicaea' as referring to a letter written by the church in Laodicaea. Why would Paul want the Colossians to read a letter from another church, especially if it was addressed to him? The Laodicaeans are meant to read the letter Paul has sent to them, and then send it on for the Colossians to read, as we can see from the expression 'that *you also* read'. Leaving that aside, the real problem is the fact that no letter addressed 'to the Laodicaeans' has survived, apart from a wretched forgery which has survived in a Latin translation. I believe that the letter 'to the Ephesians' is our missing letter, as I argue below in the notes on Eph. 1.1.

[17] 'Archippus' is referred to in Philemon 2 as Paul's 'fellow-soldier', and presumably has been appointed to some office in the church at Colossae. I believe that this instruction to make sure that Archippus is doing his job properly is light relief, a gentle leg-pull. It would be funnier if we actually knew Archippus. Perhaps he had a reputation for being over-conscientious.

[18] Paul, as is his usual custom, signs the letter which has been written by someone else to add his own personal touch. There is no reason to asssume that this is a safeguard against forgery. See my notes on Gal. 6.11 in *Reading Through Galatians* regarding this point.

'Remember my chains'; in other words, pray for me while I am in prison.

'Grace' occurs at the end of all Paul's letters.

# The Letter to the Ephesians

## Chapter 1

1 Paul, an apostle of Christ Jesus through the will of God, [sends greetings] to the saints who are (in Ephesus) and the faithful in Christ Jesus. 2 Grace to you and peace from God our Father and the Lord Jesus Christ. 3 Blessed [be] the God and Father of our Lord Jesus Christ, who blessed us with every spiritual blessing in the heavenly [places] in Christ,

[1] In some letters, such as those to the Corinthians and Thessalonians, Paul addresses his letter to the church, **têi ekklêsiâi** (or **tais ekklêsiais**, 'to the churches', as in his letter to the Galatians). In the case of the Corinthians he also adds 'to the saints', **tois hagiois**. Here, as in the letters to the Romans, Philippians and Colossians, Paul addresses his letter 'to the saints'. In all his letters, whether he addresses his audience as 'the saints' or 'the church', we are always told where they are living, 'in Rome', 'of the Thessalonians', 'of Galatia', etc. So after the words 'who are' we should expect a reference to a town or country. The strange thing about this letter is that, according to Basil,[1] the earliest copies of this letter had no such reference. Hence commentators of the early period, such as Origen, faced with no reference in the text to any town,

---

[1] *Against Eunomius*, 2.19.

explained the phrase 'the saints who are' as meaning 'those who are really saints' as distinct from ones who merely appear to be saints. 'In Ephesus' was found in some manuscripts, but Marcion the Gnostic heretic seems to have had access to a copy which had instead the phrase 'in Laodicaea'.

Because Marcion had a bad reputation for forgery amongst early scholars, it was assumed that his copy's reference to Laodicaea could be disregarded. Tertullian,[2] while claiming that it was believed that the letter was written to the Ephesians, seems to imply that standard versions of the text did not actually contain the words 'in Ephesus'. He attacks Marcion for attempting to claim that the letter was addressed to the Laodicaeans, but significantly does not claim that the standard text actually contained the words 'in Ephesus', and adds, 'the title isn't important, since the apostle has written to everybody while writing to certain individuals'. It is, however, difficult to see what Marcion could have gained by falsely claiming that this letter had originally been addressed to the church in Laodicaea, and there is no reason why we cannot take this letter to be the one referred to in Col. 4.16.

Another suggestion which has been taken up by several commentators is that the letter was circulated with a space left for the name of the town. We know that letters were circulated among the churches, but there is no evidence that letters were sent out expressly as circulars with a space for the name of the town. This suggestion became popular after it was proposed by Archbishop Ussher (1581–1656).

What is the objection to accepting the reading 'in Ephesus', since the early church fathers did believe that it was addressed to the Ephesians, although the manuscript tradition does not support them? If this letter was written to the Ephesians, it is strange that there are no personal references such as one finds in letters to churches where Paul knew several members. After

---

[2]*Against Marcion*, 5.17.

all, Paul had spent some considerable time in Ephesus and one would have expected him to mention a few names of those who were members of that church. If on the other hand the letter was addressed to the Laodicaeans, it would not be surprising if there were no references to private individuals in it, since Laodicaea was a church which Paul did not know personally.

But how did 'in Ephesus' come to be substituted for the original phrase 'in Laodicaea'? We cannot be certain of the reason, but it would appear that the church in Laodicaea fell out of favour. We can see from the references in Rev. 3.14–19 that there were serious problems in that church, serious enough for the writer to depict Christ as saying to them 'I intend to spit you out of my mouth.' The symbolic significance of deleting the name of the church can be seen in another reference in Rev. 3.5 to those who have persevered in the faith in Sardis, 'The one who conquers shall be clothed thus with white garments and I shall not wipe his name out of the book of life and I will acknowledge his name before my Father and before his angels.' As a result perhaps of some catastrophic apostasy, it would not be surprising if other churches which possessed copies of this letter deleted the reference to Laodicaea. As time went by, the need to insert a reference to some town would become obvious. Ephesus was the largest city in the area and was probably the first church to have read the letter because it was the port where the letter's carrier must have landed first. Any messenger from Paul would have been expected to report to the elders of the church in Ephesus before proceeding on his way, and it is difficult to imagine that the letter to the Laodicaeans was not eagerly read by them to the congregation in Ephesus and a copy made. So, when the original destination had been forgotten, it would not be surprising if it was assumed later that the letter had originally been addressed to them. All of this, however, is mere supposition, and in the absence of firm evidence we shall pass on.

For 'the faithful in Christ Jesus' see my notes on Col.1.2. Again, from its position in the sentence, this phrase seems to refer to Christians living elsewhere.

[2] This opening sentence is a standard Pauline formula. Note 'from God our Father and [*from*] the Lord Jesus Christ', not 'from God the Father of us and *of* the Lord Jesus Christ'. The grace and peace is from the Son as well as from the Father and the preposition 'from', **apo,** has to be taken as governing both 'God' and 'Lord'. This can be seen more clearly in Titus 1.4, which has the formula 'grace and peace from God the Father and Christ Jesus our Saviour'. Here it is grammatically impossible to translate the sentence as 'grace and peace from God the Father *of us* and *of* the Saviour Christ Jesus'.

[3] 'Who blessed' rather than 'who has blessed', because the tense of the Greek verb **eulogêsâs** is aorist, i.e. historic, not perfect. In other words, the emphasis is on the historical event of our redemption by Christ's incarnation and sacrifice, rather than the consequent and continuing blessings of the life in Christ.

'The God and Father of our Lord Jesus Christ' is rendered by some translators as 'God, the Father of our Lord Jesus Christ', but there is no reason to avoid saying that God is the God of Jesus Christ as well as our God. John 20.17 depicts the risen Christ saying, 'I am ascending to my Father and your Father, to my God and your God.' Such catholic and orthodox theologians and scholars as Theodoret and Chrysostom could see that this did not diminish the divinity of Christ. Theodoret says that the Father is God 'as of the Incarnate, but Father as of the Word of God'.

'In the heavenly [places]', **en tois epouraniois,** is a difficult phrase. Some translate it as 'among the heavenly ones' and others as 'with heavenly things', i.e. 'with spiritual blessings'. The last suggestion we can reject because it would merely repeat the idea behind the phrase 'with every spiritual blessing', **en pâsêi eulogiâi pneumatikêi.** Paul uses the adjective **epouranios** five times in I Corinthians, but the phrase **en tois epouraniois** is only found in this letter, where it occurs five times. When we examine the other cases in this letter where the phrase is used, it seems more likely that it refers to locality than persons. This is particularly so in 3.10 and 6.12. The obvious meaning is that our spiritual blessings are located in heaven, that is, they are permanent and not transitory. If we add 'which is' after 'blessing', this meaning becomes even clearer. Many commentators stop at this point, but there is another and profounder meaning here. We have ourselves been transported into heaven, as we see from the statement in 2.6, 'and he raised us together and seated us together in the heavenly places in Christ Jesus', and from Col. 1.13, 'and transported us to the kingdom of his dear son'. As Lightfoot comments, 'It is the heaven which lies within and about the true Christian.' Hence it is also possible to take the phrase **en Christôi**, translated here 'in Christ', as meaning '*with* Christ'.

4 seeing that he chose us in him before the foundation of the world to be holy and blameless before his face in love, 5 having ordained us beforehand for adoption by him through Jesus Christ according to the good pleasure of his will, 6 to the praise of the glory of his grace, [the grace] with which he favoured us in his beloved.

[4] 'In him', **en autôi**, refers to Christ. God the Father is the subject of the verb 'he chose'. Christ is the means through which God adopted us, as is made clear in the next verse. Indeed, verses 3, 4, 5, 6 and 7 all make the same points in different ways: firstly, that Christ is the means whereby we have been saved, and secondly, that it is all due to God's grace. Verses 4 and 5 also add a third point, namely, that it was decided by God beforehand.

'Holy and blameless'; see the notes on Col. 1.22.

'Before his face', **katenôpion autou**, as also in Col. 1.22, refers to the presence of God.

'In love' traditionally has been taken to be God's love for us, but some commentators argue, usually because of the Greek word order, that it is our love for God, and translate the last part as 'holy and blameless in love before him'. For instance, the NEB has 'to be dedicated, to be without blemish in his sight, to be full of love'. But since the whole of this passage is a tribute to God's grace and love in choosing us to be his own children, it seems perverse to argue that the love referred to here could be our love for him. Although Chrysostom takes the phrase 'in love' with the verb **proörisâs**, 'having ordained beforehand' in the next verse, it is obvious that he also took the love referred to here as being God's love and not ours. The Greek word order is slightly unusual but is simply due to the emphasis – 'God chose us and he did so because he *loves* us.'

[5] This verse is a restatement in different terms of the theme of the previous verse and is a typical example of Paul's legalistic way of arguing. Saying the same thing in a different way is characteristic of a lawyer. Such repetitions can puzzle those commentators who forget Paul's background.

'By him', **eis auton**, literally, 'into him', refers this time to God, not Christ.

'According to the good pleasure', **kata tên eudokiân**, is repeated in v. 9. Paul is emphasizing the fact that our salvation is not due to some choice or any merit on our part but is a free gift of grace on God's part. He is also obliquely making another point, i.e. that God's purposes are inscrutable.

[6] 'To the praise of the glory' is repeated in vv. 12 and 14 and is best taken in parenthesis as a spontaneous expression of praise and adoration, namely, a short praise formula.

'Favoured', **echaritôsen**, from the verb **charitoô**, is only found in one other passage in the NT, Luke 1.28, where it is used by the angel Gabriel in his salutation of Mary. Some commentators stress the act of grace on God's part in favouring us and shy away from the notion that someone who has been graced by God is consequently full of grace. As Chrysostom points out, 'he has not only freed us from sin, but actually made us loveable (**eperastous**) . . . It is as if one were to take a leper and change him into a lovely youth.' Incidentally, we miss the word-play with this verb and the noun 'grace', **charis**. Perhaps we should translate the last part as 'the grace with which he has graced us'. For a fuller discussion of the meaning of **charis** see my notes on Gal. 1.3 and Heb. 12.28 in this series.

'His beloved', **tôi êgapêmenôi**, as a way of referring to Christ, is more characteristic of John's style than Paul's. Perhaps it was a popular way of referring to Jesus in the province of Asia, and Paul is using an idiom which would appeal to his audience.

7 In him we have our redemption through his blood, the forgiveness of our sins, according to the wealth of his grace, 8 which he poured out abundantly on us with all wisdom and judgment, 9 making known to us the secret of his will, according to his good pleasure which he displayed in him,

[7] For 'redemption' see the notes on Col. 1.14. This verse differs from the Colossians verse by the addition of 'through his blood', which makes clear how the ransom was paid, and by the use of **paraptômatôn** instead of **hamartiôn** for 'of sins'. See the notes below on 2.1 regarding the latter. The NEB 'our release is secured' is weak on two counts: firstly, there is no mention of payment, and secondly, it gives the impression that our release has merely been guaranteed and has not happened yet.

[8] 'Poured out abundantly', **eperisseusen**, from a verb which occurs also in Col. 2.7, 'overflowing', **perisseuontes**. In other words, 'lavished'.

'Wisdom and judgment', **sophiâi kai phronêsei**, are what we receive from God, not what he displays in bestowing his grace

on us. Aristotle (*Nicomachean Ethics*, 1141a, 18) defines
**sophiâ** as 'intellect and knowledge, knowledge, so to speak, of
the most precious things, with a head on it'. **Phronêsis** is to do
with 'human matters and things about which one can deliberate'. This is echoed by Philo (*On Rewards and Punishments*,
14) where he speaks of wisdom as 'to do with the service of
God', and judgment as 'to do with the management of human
life'.

[9] 'Secret of his will', **mystêrion tou thelêmatos autou;** see
note on Col. 1.26.

'Which he displayed in him', rather than 'which he had
purposed in himself', as some commentators suggest. The verb
**protithemai** is very common in the sense of 'display', 'show',
'lay out', 'notify publicly' or 'propose'. It can also mean
'advance' (money). The sense here is that God displayed or
embodied his good pleasure by giving us his Son.

10 so that, in the dispensation of the fullness of the
times, he might sum up in Christ everything in heaven
and earth, in him 11 in whom we have also been
allotted a portion, having been ordained beforehand
according to the proposing of the one who works
everything according to the determination of his will,
12 so that we should be, to the praise of his glory, the
ones who were first to place our hope in Christ.

[10] 'Dispensation', **oikonomiân**, literally, 'management of a
household' or 'stewardship'. God had a management plan for
the salvation of mankind which was revealed when the time
was right.

'Of the fullness of the times', **tou plêrômatos tôn kairôn**, in
other words, 'when the time of fulfilment had come'. Compare
Gal. 4.4, 'But when *the time of fulfilment* (**to plêrôma tou
chronou**) came, God sent out his son.'

'Sum up', **anakephalaiôsasthai**, contains the root **kephalê**, 'head'. So everything is summed up under one heading and, at the same time, placed under one Head, i.e. Christ. Chrysostom explains the verb as meaning 'to join together' and goes on to say, 'he has brought everyone under one *head*' (**kephalên**). The Vulgate uses the word *instaurare*, 'to restore'. Clearly, in this verse there are several ideas in the writer's mind. Firstly, the final goal of creation has been reached; secondly, everything has been united and harmonized; thirdly, the universe has been healed and restored; and fourthly, Christ has been placed as Head above all.

[11] 'We have also' rather than 'we too', since we do not have the pronoun **hêmeis**, 'we', which would have put the emphasis on 'we'.

'Allotted a portion', **eklêrôthêmen**, from the noun **klêros**, 'a lot'. The verb **klêroô** meant originally 'I appoint by lot' and was used to describe the casting of lots in the appointment of magistrates by political assemblies. Some translate 'chosen as his lot', but there is no evidence for this usage. It is possible to see how the appointing of magistrates by the casting of lots can be seen as analogous to the selection of those God wishes to save. The Vulg. *sorte vocati sumus* unfortunately gives the impression that there is something random about the process, i.e. 'we have been called by chance'.

'Ordained beforehand', **proöristhentes**, picks up the **proörisâs** of v. 5.

'According to', **kata**, is used twice in the same verse, and I have kept the repetition although it is stylistically unfortunate.

'Proposing', **prothesin**, is the noun from the verb **pro-tithemai**, 'I display', used in v. 9.

'According to the determination', **kata tên boulên**, is a synonym for 'according to the good pleasure', **kata tên eudok-iân**, of vv 5 and 9.

[12] I have taken the phrase 'to the praise of his glory' as being

in parenthesis, as it is elsewhere in this chapter, but some commentators take it as the complement of the verb and translate, 'so that we, who were the first to place our hope in Christ, should be to the praise of his glory'. The writer, however, is making the point that he, together with his fellow *Jewish* Christians, was the first to accept Christ, since he goes on to speak of the *Gentile* Christians accepting Christ in the next verse. A similar sentiment is expressed in Romans (1.16; 2.9, 10): 'the Jew first, and [then] also the Greek', and also in 15.8, 9, 'For I say that Christ was made a minister of the circumcision for God's truth, in order to confirm the promises of our fathers, and that the Gentiles might glorify God for his mercy.'

13 in whom you, too, when you heard the word of truth, the good news of your salvation, in whom, when you too believed, you were sealed with the Holy Spirit of the promise, 14 which is a down payment of our inheritance, for the redemption of [our] acquisition, to the praise of his glory.

[13] Several commentators feel the need to supply a verb with 'in whom you too . . .', such as 'hoped' or 'obtained an inherit-ance', but it is best to take the second 'in whom' as a rhetorical repetition of the first one and both as going with 'you were sealed'. The commercial language of these verses should be noted. 'Sealing' is marking goods with the seal of the owner before consignment.

'The promise' is that which was given to Abraham by God, and which is passed on to those justified by faith in Christ. See the notes on 2.12. Galatians and Hebrews discuss this subject in great detail. Paul is reminding the Gentile Christians that they are the heirs of the promise and true descendants of Abraham.

[14] 'Down payment', **arrabôn,** another commercial word, is a Semitic term which passed into Greek, probably from the Phoenician traders. Paul is saying that we have already received the gift of the Holy Spirit as a deposit – the full gift of the inheritance promised to us is still to come. II Cor. 1.22 is very reminiscent of this passage, 'who has also *sealed* us and given us the *down payment* of the Spirit in our hearts'. NEB, 'and that Spirit is the pledge that we shall enter upon our heritage', obscures the fact that we have actually received the Spirit already as part of our inheritance. Clement of Alexandria (*Excerpts from the Prophetic Scriptures*, 12) says, 'we have not gained everything nor are we entirely without, but have received, as it were, a *down payment* (**arrabôna**) of everlasting benefits and our Father's treasure'.

'Acquisition', **peripoiêseôs** (AV 'purchased possession'), is the property which is to be inherited by us, the 'better and enduring property' of Heb. 10.34, the pledge which we shall redeem (note the use of the term 'redemption', **apolytrôsin,** which this time refers not to us being redeemed, but to us redeeming our property). This interpretation seems to be supported by the Vulg. *in redemptionem adquisitionis.* But some translators, such as the NEB, which has 'when God has redeemed what is his own', interpret the term **peripoiêseôs** as a reference to us as the property of God, i.e. God's possession. Such interpretations, however, would need the addition of **tou Theou,** 'God's'. Furthermore, they do not fit the argument of the rest of this passage which is clearly referring to the benefits accruing to the believer. After all, a down payment is given to those who are going to receive the rest of the property at a later date. For this to be God's possession, God would have had to receive the down payment. **Peripoiêsis,** incidentally, is another of those words which some commentators claim carry a different sense in Ephesians from that which they carry elsewhere. It is difficult, however, to see how its use here to denote a concrete acquisition differs materially from its use in I Thess. 5.9 or II Thess. 2.14 to denote the act of acquiring. See also my note on Heb. 10.39 in *Reading Through Hebrews*.

'To the praise of his glory' again is in parenthesis. See note on v. 6.

15 For this reason, I, too, hearing of the faith in the Lord Jesus [that is] amongst you and the love [you show] to all the saints, 16 do not cease giving thanks for you, mentioning you in my prayers, 17 that the God of our Lord Jesus Christ, the Father of Glory, may give you the spirit of wisdom and revelation in the knowledge of him,

[15] What is 'this reason'? The fact that his audience has also been sealed by the Spirit and given the inheritance.

'Hearing' implies either that Paul did not know this group of Christians personally, or that he had not seen them for some time.

'The love', **tên agapên**, is not found in some good manuscripts but it seems necessary here. The Vulgate *dilectionem* clearly is based on a text which had **agapên**.

[16] 'Mentioning you', literally 'making mention of you'. Most manuscripts do not have **hûmôn**, 'of you', which is found in a few texts, but the meaning is clear without it.

[17] 'The spirit of wisdom and revelation' can be paraphrased as 'the spiritual gifts of wisdom and the ability to reveal'.

'In the knowledge of him', **en epignôsei autou**, is knowing *about* Christ rather than knowledge given *by* him, i.e. 'his knowledge'. From comparing similar phrases elsewhere in the NT, such as II Tim. 2.25; 3.7, 'knowledge of the truth', and Rom. 3.20, 'knowledge of sin', we can be fairly sure that this is the meaning here. **Epignôsis** is also 'recognition' (of a person), as I point out in my notes on Col. 1.9.

18 with the eyes of your hearts enlightened, to know what is the hope of his calling, and what is the wealth of the glory of his inheritance among the saints, 19 and what is the surpassing greatness of his power towards us who believe, according to the action of the might of his strength,

[18] The metaphor of 'the eyes of your heart[s]' is reminiscent of 'the eye of the soul', **to tês psûchês omma**, of Platonism (*Republic* 533D), where it denotes the inner understanding which gives one true knowledge in contrast to the sense which can only perceive material things.

'Enlightened', **pephôtismenous**, often stands for 'baptized'. [A note for those with some Greek: we would expect the construction 'enlightened' (dative referring to 'you') '*as to* the eyes' (accusative of respect), but this participle is accusative and so cannot go with the dative 'you' of the previous verse. It is probably best to take it as describing 'eyes' and the whole phrase as another object of the verb 'give'.]

'The hope of his calling' is 'the hope to which he has called you'. Clearly this verse is referring to the future joys awaiting the faithful believer. This is echoed by 'the wealth of the glory of his inheritance', i.e the glorious riches (and the rich glory) they will inherit. 'Wealth of glory' also occurs in 3.16 and Col. 1.27 and in Rom. 9.23. There is no reason to take 'his inheritance among the saints' as meaning 'the inheritance God has in his saints'. Paul's remarks to the elders of the church in Ephesus (Acts 20.32) are particularly relevant: 'I commend you to God and to the word of his grace which can build you up and give you the *inheritance amongst all those who have been sanctified.*'

[19] This verse and the next one reassure the audience by emphasizing that God's power, which was manifested by raising Christ from the dead, will also raise them from physical

death, just as he has already resurrected them from the death of sin in baptism. See Col. 2.12, 13, 'buried with him in that baptism, in which you were also raised together [with him] through your faith in the action of God who raised him from the dead, and while you were dead in your sins . . . he brought you to life together with him.' God's power has already been manifested, and it *will be* manifested by our resurrection at the end.

'Who believe', **tous pisteuontas**, a present participle, i.e. 'continuing to believe'. Paul is making the point that it is not enough to have believed once and committed oneself to Christ; one must go on believing and being faithful.

The emphasis in this verse on God's power is reinforced by four different words: **dynameôs**, 'power'; **energeian**, 'action'; **kratous**, 'might'; **ischyos**, 'strength'. **Dynamis** is the ability to do anything and is often used in the NT to denote 'miracle', or 'act of power', e.g. II Cor. 12.12; Heb. 2.4. See in my *Reading Through Galatians* the notes on 3.5. For **energeia** see notes on Col. 1.29. **Kratos** is supremacy or mastery, i.e. power over someone or something, as in Heb.2.14, where the devil is described as having the 'power (**kratos**) of death'. **Ischys** is strength, often in a physical sense, or inherent power.

20 [the action] which he performed in Christ by raising him from the dead and seating him at his right hand in the heavenly [places], 21 above every rule, authority, power and lordship and every name that can be named, not only in this world but in the world to come;

[20] The significance of 'seating him at his right hand' is that Christ was raised above all other powers and authorities. The writer of the letter to the Hebrews alludes five times to Christ's seat at the right hand of God. See my note on 10.12 in *Reading Through Hebrews*.

See the notes on 'in the heavenly [places]' in v. 3.

[21] What are these powers? It is clear from the parallel passage in Col. 1.16 that Paul is referring to both angelic and earthly, i.e. human, powers. Because the 'world to come' of this passage seems to answer to the 'heaven' of Colossians, and 'this world' to the 'earth', we could say that Paul is thinking of both time and place – 'not only here but there; not only now but then'. There has been a great deal of speculation about the distinctions between the terms used here. Seven orders of spiritual powers were identified by some early writers, the two highest being thrones and authorities, while Origen spoke of five classes, ranging from angels to lordships, but we should heed Chrysostom and Augustine, who discourage such speculation. The latter's comment is worth repeating: 'let those who can speak do so, if, indeed, they can prove what they are saying; I, for my part, admit I know nothing of these matters.'

'Name that can be named', **onomatos onomazomenou** is the equivalent of 'person that can be identified'. The use of 'name' as a synonym of 'person' can be seen in Acts 1.15, 'a crowd of around a hundred and twenty *persons* (**onomatôn**)'.

22 and 'he has subjected all things beneath his feet' and given him as head above all things to the church, 23 which is his body, the fulfilment of him who is being fulfilled in every respect in everything.

[22] The quotation from Ps. 8.6 is also used in I Cor. 15.27 and Heb. 2.8 to stress the supremacy of Christ over all creation.

For 'head', see the note on Col. 1.18. 'Above all things' adds a further dimension: Christ is the head of all creation, not just of the church. Chrysostom sees the implication of this for the church: 'He has raised up the church as though by a crane to a great height and sat her on that throne; for where the head is, there is the body also.'

[23] This verse is not easy to understand, as one can see by comparing the various translations of the passage. NEB, for example, even offers three different paraphrases. Most of the difficulty arises from the verb 'is being fulfilled'. Several commentators translate this passive participle **plêroumenou** as though it had an active sense, 'fulfilling', i.e. 'who fulfils'. Then there is the ambiguity of the verb itself, which can carry at least five meanings: 'fill', 'fulfil', 'complete', 'perfect' and 'finish'. Thirdly, we have the related noun 'fulfilment', **plêrôma**, which I discuss in the notes on Col. 1.19. Finally, we have the phrase 'in every respect in everything', literally, 'all things in all [things]', **ta panta en pâsin**, which again is hard to define.

Let us start by rejecting the suggestion that the participle **plêroumenou** can be treated as having an active sense, in other words, as a middle voice, although it has a passive form. For those not familiar with Greek grammar, I would explain that the middle roughly corresponds to the Latin deponent verb, which looks passive but is actually active. The verb **plêroô** is used 86 times in the NT, and not once do we find an example of it being used in the middle voice. In short, it is most unlikely that the verb here means 'fulfils' or 'fills'. It must mean 'is being fulfilled/filled'. Jerome specifically says that it is passive, '*patientis est verbum*', and goes on to compare the situation with that of an emperor who is increased when his army grows and when he gains new provinces and new peoples. The Vulg. also uses a passive, *adimpletur*, to translate the verb.

The reason why so many commentators cling to the notion that Christ is the one who fulfils is that they have difficulty in accepting the idea that Christ needs anything to make him complete. Paul, however, is expressing the amazing paradox that he who needs nothing, needs his church to fulfil him. Of course, the church also needs Christ – she could not exist without him; but that is not what this verse is saying. Chrysostom, along with other early scholars, had no difficulty with the concept that Christ needed his church in order to be complete. He also recognized that the church was the **plêrôma**, 'fulfilment', of Christ, not the other way round. In other words, the Greek **tou**, 'of him who', should not be taken here as meaning 'coming from him'. Even Lightfoot found it difficult to believe that the church could give Christ something that would make *him* complete. He said, 'all the divine graces which reside in Him are imparted to her; His fullness is communicated to her; and thus she may be said to be his **plêrôma**'. Chrysostom deserves to be quoted at length: 'He (Paul) says **plêrôma** just as the head is completed by the body, for the body is composed of all the parts and has need of each one. See how he (Paul) brings him (Christ) in as needing all. For unless we be many, and one a hand, another a foot, and another some other part, the whole body is not completed. By all, then, is his body completed. Then the head is completed, then the body becomes perfect, when we are all joined and united together.'

The tense of the participle **plêroumenou** is also significant. Paul uses the present because he sees the fulfilment as a continuing process. We can now understand the significance of the phrase 'in every respect in everything'. Just as Christ is the head of his church, so he is the head of the whole of creation, which is in the process of being redeemed and renewed. When all is complete and the whole of creation is made new in Christ, then Christ's work is finished.

# Chapter 2

1 And while you were dead in your sins and transgressions, 2 in which you once lived your lives in accordance with the age of this world, in accordance with the ruler of the power of the air, the spirit who is now at work in the children of disobedience,

[1] Note that this verse has no main verb. Paul, as we see in other letters, often interrupts himself with a digression, then when he returns to his theme assumes a different object or fails to make the grammar fit. The main verb governing the object 'you' in this verse is 'brought to life' in v. 5, where it is used with another object, 'us'.

'Sins', **paraptômasin**, and 'transgressions', **hamartiais**, according to Jerome, differ in that the former are the beginnings of sin in thought while the latter are the actual sinful deeds. Augustine regarded the former as sins of thoughtlessness and the latter as deliberate sins. Paul, however, probably does not intend to differentiate between them, as we can see when we compare Col. 1.14 and its parallel Eph. 1.7, where Colossians has **hamartiôn** and Ephesians **paraptômatôn**. He also seems to use them as synonyms in Rom. 5.20, 'The Law came in so that that the transgression (**paraptôma**) might be in excess; but where sin (**hamartiâ**) was excessive, grace was super-abundant.'

[2] 'In accordance with the age of this world', **kata ton aiôna tou kosmou toutou,** that is, conforming to the spirit of the age we live in. **Aiôn** is 'age', 'era' or 'world'. **Kosmos** also can mean 'world', but usually in a spatial sense, i.e. the created material world, while **aiôn** denotes the temporal aspect of 'world'.

'The ruler of the power of the air' is the spiritual power that operates in the world. **Aêr**, as distinct from the **aethêr**, is the lower atmosphere. Some commentators have suggested that 'air' in this context is to be understood in the sense of 'mist' and hence 'darkness', but there is no need to stretch the meaning so far. The air was believed by both pagans and Jews to be full of spirits.

For 'children of disobedience' see notes on Col. 3.6.

3 amongst whom we, too, all lived once in the desires of our flesh, doing whatever our flesh and our minds wanted, and we were by nature children of anger just like the rest, 4 but God, being rich in mercy, through the great love he had for us, 5 and while we were dead in our sins, brought us to life together with Christ – by grace you have been saved –

[3] 'We', i.e. Paul and other Jewish Christians, is a better reading than the 'you' found in some manuscripts. The expression 'by nature', **physei,** is used by Paul in Gal. 2.15 speaking of Peter and himself, 'We are Jews *by nature*, **physei,** and not Gentile sinners.' Here, too, Paul must be referring to those who were born into Judaism. 'Just like the rest', therefore, refers to the Gentiles, not the rest of the Jews.

'Children of anger', another Hebraism like that in the previous verse. They are those human beings who deserve God's condemnation.

[4] 'Through the great love he had for us', literally, 'because of the much love of his [with] which he loved us'.

[5] This verse picks up from v. 1, but note the shift from 'you' to 'we'.

'And while we were dead', not 'even when were dead', as some translations have it. 'And' here is acting as a conjunction, not as an emphasizing word.

'Brought . . . to life together with Christ', **synezôöpoiêsen tôi Christôi**, links our resurrection with that of Christ. God, as Chrysostom says, 'made both him and us alive'. Some manuscripts have **en**, 'in', in front of 'Christ', which would alter this verse to mean that God brought to life Gentiles and Jews together, a new point which he makes in the next verse.

'By grace you have been saved', a characteristic spontaneous interjection by Paul stressing that our salvation was an act of grace on God's part, because of his mercy and love, and not something we earned by good behaviour.

6 and raised us together and seated us together in the heavenly places in Christ Jesus, 7 in order to show in the coming ages the surpassing wealth of his grace in his kindness towards us in Christ Jesus. 8 For you have been saved by grace through faith; and this [does] not [come] from you [but is] a gift of God; 9 [it does] not [come] from works, lest anyone should boast.

[6] '*In* Christ Jesus', where we would have expected '*with* Christ Jesus'. There is a reason for this; Paul is developing the theme of the previous verse. The process of redemption works because all believers, both Jew and Gentile, are incorporated together in Christ. The verbs **synêgeiren**, 'raised together', and **synekathisen**, 'seated together', refer not only to the redeemed being raised together with Christ but to their being raised together with each other, i.e. Jew and Gentile together with Christ. They are members of the same body and Christ is joined to them as the head of that same body. The use of the **syn**-prefix, which we have already noted in Col. 1.17; 2.12, 13, is

picked up again in 3.6, 'the Gentiles are *joint* heirs, belong to a *joint* body and are *joint* sharers in the promise in Christ Jesus through the gospel'. See also the notes on 4.16.

Note the amazing statement that the redeemed have already been raised up and seated in heaven. The verbs do not refer to a future event but to one that has already taken place. Some modern commentators have difficulty accepting the obvious meaning of this verse. For example, Thompson explains away the verse as follows: 'Therefore, to be in union with Christ Jesus means to be raised up and enthroned with Jesus *in the sense of being committed to the God-centred way of life.*'

[7] 'In the coming ages', **en tois aiôsin tois eperchomenois**, simply means 'in the future' or 'in the world to come'. There is no reason to take this phrase as indicating that the writer thought that a long succession of eras would pass before Christ returned to earth. The phrase is meant to suggest the infinite nature of the eternal kingdom and of the inheritance awaiting the faithful.

[8, 9] Is the 'gift of God' faith, or the salvation that comes through faith? It must be the latter. Firstly the word 'this' is neuter, referring to the verb, not feminine, which would have to refer to 'faith', **pistis**. More seriously, we can prove from many other passages in Paul's letters that the phrase 'from works' is only found in a context where he is discussing the question whether salvation, or justification, can come 'from works' or 'from faith'. In other words, this gift of God must come 'from faith', if it does not come 'from works'. Therefore, if we assume that 'faith' is the gift of God referred to here, it would have to come 'from faith', which is absurd. As Theophylact says, 'He does not call faith the gift of God, but salvation through faith – this is the gift of God.' Of course, faith is also a gift from God, like everything else, but that is not what Paul is saying here.

10 For we are his handiwork created in Christ Jesus with a view to the good works for which God prepared [us] beforehand, so that we should live lives devoted to them. 11 Therefore, remember that you, who were once Gentiles in the flesh, called the uncircumcision by those called the circumcision in the flesh made by hands, 12 that you were at that time separated from Christ, excluded from the citizenship of Israel and strangers to the covenants of the promise, with no hope and without God in the world.

[10] 'For which God prepared [us] beforehand' or 'which God prepared beforehand'. The Vulg. *quae praeparavit Deus* supports the latter, but it is easier to take 'us' as the unstated object of the verb, since the relative pronoun is a dative, **hois**, not an accusative. Hence '*for* which'. Furthermore, it fits the statement 'for we are his handiwork' better if we take it that God prepared us rather than the good works.

'Live lives devoted to them', literally, 'walk in them'.

[11] '*Once* Gentiles in the flesh' implies that they no longer are Gentiles in that sense. Similarly, 'those *called* the circumcision' are not really the circumcised. 'In the flesh' is contrasted with the unstated 'in the spirit'. Those who were once the uncircumcised in a material sense are now those who are spiritually circumcised, and *vice versa*.

[12] 'Excluded', **apêllotriômenoi,** as in Col. 1.21. See notes on that verse.

'The covenants of the promise' refer to the covenant made by God with Abraham when God promised that he would be the father of many nations (Gen. 17.4–6), that he would be given a new homeland (Gen. 12.1–2), and particularly that all the nations of the earth would be blessed through him (Gen. 22.16–18). These promises originally were only valid for those who were circumcised and kept the Law, but now through Christ they have been extended to the Gentile believers in Christ. See Gal. 3.6–18 and Heb. 6.13–20 for more on this subject.

There is a close connection between 'separated from Christ' and 'strangers to the covenants of the promise'. The promise given to Abraham and his descendants was only fulfilled by Christ, and so it is only by faith in Christ that we can gain the promise given to Abraham. Paul is not saying 'you were *not only* without Christ, *but also* without the promise given to Abraham', since the one depends on the other. Chrysostom rightly takes this verse as referring both to the heavenly and the earthly Israel. It certainly cannot be taken purely in a material sense.

'Without God', **atheoi**, i.e. abandoned by God or not knowing God, not 'atheists'.

13 But now, in Christ Jesus, you who were once distant have been made near by the blood of Christ. 14 For he is our peace, he who made both one and destroyed the barrier of the enclosure, the hostility by his flesh, 15 having abolished the Law of the commandments with its decrees, in order to build the two into one new person in him by making peace, 16 and reconcile again the two to God in one body through the cross, having killed the hostility by it.

[13] 'Near', i.e. in the household of Israel. The rabbis speak of 'bringing near' when they refer to a proselyte being admitted into full membership of the Jewish community. Paul, of course, is referring to the true Israel of the new covenant.

[14] Christ has brought about peace not only between Jew and Gentile, but also between mankind and God.

'The barrier of the enclosure', **to mesotoichon tou**

**phragmou**, the physical barrier which separated the Court of the Gentiles from the Court of Israel in the Temple at Jerusalem, is used here as a symbol of the 'hostility' that separated Jew from Gentile. See Col. 1.21. As we know from inscriptions which have been excavated on the site, the death penalty was threatened for any Gentile who went beyond the barrier. It is ironic that Paul's imprisonment was the result of an accusation that he had taken a Gentile, Trophimus an Ephesian, into an area of the Temple that was forbidden to Gentiles.

'By his flesh', as I point out in the notes to Col. 1.22, refers to Christ's incarnation and sacrifice. It also anticipates v. 16, where Paul refers to Christ's body, the church, in which he has made us all one. Chrysostom, referring to making 'both one', **ta amphotera hen**, graphically comments, 'as if one should melt down a statue of silver and another of lead, and the two should come out gold'.

[15] 'Having abolished', **katargêsâs**, a typically Pauline term from a verb that can also mean 'cancel', 'make redundant', or 'nullify'.

'Law of the commandments with its decrees' is the Mosaic Law. In Jewish terminology it might be described as the *Torah* and *Mitzvah*, 'the Law and Commandment'. God is supposed to have revealed 613 *mitzvot* to Moses on Sinai. They are recorded in the five books of Moses, i.e. the Pentateuch, and consist of the statutes regulating ritual performances, that is, obligations to God, and the judgments covering matters affecting human beings, such as laws dealing with murder and theft. The Greek word used in this verse for 'decrees' is **dogmasin**, a word used also in Col. 2.14, that denotes judgments, ordinances and particularly judicial or legislative decisions. There is no warrant for taking **en dogmasin** as meaning 'by his decrees', i.e. Christ's laws, and translating the verse as though it referred to Christ abolishing the Law by means of his own laws. See the notes on Col. 2.14.

'Build' refers forward to the metaphor of the church as a building in vv. 20–22. This is clear from the use of the word **ktisêi**, which means 'build' or 'found' as well as 'create', Vulg. *condat*.

'Into one new person/man', **eis hena kainon anthrôpon**, picked up again in 4.24, echoes the 'new creation', **kainê ktisis**, of II Cor. 5.17 and Gal. 6.15. Rom. 6.6 speaks of the opposite, **ho palaios hêmôn anthrôpos**, 'our old person/man'. See also notes on 4.13 and Col. 3.10.

[16] This verse is packed with meaning and needs careful examination to reveal its subtlety. For instance, the phrase 'in one body' can be taken in two ways. Firstly, it refers to the body of Christ sacrificed on the cross, the one body through which the world was saved. Secondly, it refers to the body of the church which as the body of Christ also died on the cross, the one body of which all Christians are members. We have been crucified with Christ, and as we have shared in his death we share in his resurrection. As Gal. 2.19 says, 'I have been crucified along with Christ', and Rom.6.6 speaks of 'our old person' as being crucified with him. Similarly, the argument of Gal. 3.27, 28 is that Jew and Gentile are one in Christ because they have both been baptized into Christ.

Then we have the double sense of reconciliation, of humanity to God, 'reconcile the two to God', and of Jew to Gentile, having 'killed the hostility'. For 'reconcile *again*', see note on Col. 1.20. 'The hostility', **tên echthrân**, can be '*their*' hostility', i.e. the hostility between Jew and Gentile and the hostility both of them displayed to God, as well as God's hostility towards both of them in their unredeemed state.

'By it', or as the AV has it, 'thereby', i.e. by the cross rather than 'in (or 'by') him'. See Col. 2.15.

17 He came and preached the gospel of peace to you who were distant and peace to those who were near, 18 since we both have through him our introduction to the Father in one Spirit. 19 So then, you are no longer

strangers and aliens but fellow citizens with the saints, and members of God's household, 20 built up on the foundation of the apostles and prophets, with Christ Jesus himself as the corner stone, 21 on which the whole building is fitted together and grows into a holy temple in the Lord, 22 and on which you, too, are being built up together into a dwelling place of God in the spirit.

[17] 'He came', i.e. into the world, **eis ton kosmon**, as St John usually adds. It refers to Christ coming in the flesh when he was born, i.e. his incarnation. Some modern commentators interpret the expression as Christ coming in the spirit and preaching the gospel through his apostles after his ascension. Hodge thinks that it refers to Christ's appearance after his death. 'He came', however, seems an unlikely way of referring to the resurrection or the post-Pentecostal presence, without some extra phrase, such as 'having died' or 'having ascended'. 'Come' is generally applied to Christ in reference either to his incarnation or his second coming. Furthermore, 'preached', **euêngelisato**, must refer to Christ's earthly ministry; it can hardly be preaching by proxy, as the first interpretation demands, nor, following Hodge's hypothesis, does it seem an appropriate term to describe the resurrected Christ's message to his disciples.

'You who were distant' are the Gentiles, and 'those who were near' are the Jews (see note on v. 13). The clear implication is that Christ actually preached to Gentiles as well as Jews, and a careful reading of the Gospel accounts of Christ's ministry shows this was so. Paul is reminding his audience that Christ himself wanted the Gentiles to be included in his church – it is not just an afterthought of apostles like himself, as his enemies, contemporary or modern, might have suggested.

Note the repetition of 'peace'. It is not just peace between God and his church, but peace between Jews and Gentiles, a peace which both parties must display to each other. The emphasis on 'both' is spelled out in the next verse.

[18] This is a subtle statement regarding the relationship between Father, Son and Holy Spirit. The Son introduces us *to* the Father *in* the Spirit.

'Introduction', **prosagôgên**, as Chrysostom points out, is not-'access', as the AV translates. 'He (Paul) did not say **prosodon** (access) but **prosagôgên** (introduction); for we did not approach by ourselves, but were introduced by him (Christ).' **Prosagôgê** is the word used to describe the act of a chamberlain who introduces someone into the presence of a king. The verb **prosagô** is used in I Peter 3.18 in this sense, 'in order to *introduce* (**prosagagêi**) you to God'.


[19] 'So then', **ara oun**, is an expression used eleven times by Paul elsewhere in the NT, and by no one else. It would be a clever forger who knew that.

'Strangers', **xenoi**, are foreigners in general, while 'aliens', **paroikoi**, are resident foreigners.

'Saints' are those who belong to the heavenly Jerusalem. They include the faithful of the OT, as we know from the letter to the Hebrews (see my note on 12.23 in *Reading Through Hebrews*). Chrysostom mentions Abraham, Moses and Elias as examples of such 'saints'. Some modern commentators, however, prefer to restrict this category to specifically Christian converts.

Note the comma after 'saints'. 'With' only goes with 'saints', not 'members', which is nominative, like 'fellow citizens'.

'Members of God's household', **oikeioi tou Theou**, is the opposite of 'those outside', **hoi exô**, which is used in Col. 4.5 and elsewhere to refer to non-believers.


[20] 'Built up on . . .', **epoikodomêthentes epi . . .**, Vulg. *super-aedificati super*, carries the sense of building something in addition to what has already been built, that is, in addition to the foundations and the corner stone.

The meaning of 'the foundation of the apostles and prophets' is not immediately apparent. There are four interpretations of the phrase 'of the apostles and prophets':

1. Laid by the apostles and prophets,
2. On which the apostles and prophets build,
3. On which the apostles and prophets have been built,
4. Which consists of the apostles and prophets.

Chrysostom rightly preferred the fourth interpretation. Since Christ is the corner stone, the apostles and prophets must be the foundation. We might add that the third interpretation is wrong because it would imply that somebody else was the foundation; the second inappropriate because, presumably, they do not continue to build when they have died; and the first is incorrect because God is the one who lays the foundation.

The next question is to identify the prophets. Are they only those referred to in the NT, or do they include OT patriarchs, such as Isaiah or Amos? We know from other passages in the NT that the term 'apostles and prophets' often refers to contemporary members of the church. See, for example, Luke 11.49, and in this letter, 3.5 and 4.11. But at the same time, such passages as Acts 10.43, 'the prophets bear witness to him, that everyone who believes in him shall receive forgiveness of sins through his name', and Acts 3.24, 'and all the prophets from Samuel and his successors who have spoken [of these things], have also announced these days', clearly indicate the importance of the OT prophets in establishing the the gospel of Christ. Hence it is possible to take 'prophets' here as referring to both the new and the old prophets. John the Baptist would also be included in this company.

'Himself', rather than 'of it', i.e. of the building. The Greek word **autou** carries both meanings.

'Corner stone', **akrogôniaiou**, 'the head of the corner', not the 'keystone', which is used at the top of an arch, but the stone which determines to a large extent the general position and layout of the building, what we might call the 'foundation stone'. The reference is to Isa. 28.16 (AV), 'Behold, I lay in Zion for a foundation a stone, a tried stone, a precious corner stone, a sure foundation.'

[21] 'On which', or 'in whom', **en hôi.**

'The whole building', **pâsa oikodomê.** Because the definite article has been omitted, it has been argued by Abbott that this phrase can only mean 'every building'. Since this obviously does not make sense in this context, it has been suggested that 'building' here actually means 'part of the building', but there is no need to find an ingenious solution to a problem which does not exist. It is certainly true that in classical Greek 'all the' or 'the whole' would normally demand the definite article, since **pâs(a)** without the article generally means 'each' or 'every'. In other words, we would expect **pâsa hê oikodomê,** or **hê pâsa oikodomê,** but there are other examples of the omission of the article. For example, Acts 2.36, **pâs oikos Israêl,** 'the whole household of Israel'; Acts 7.22, **en pâsêi sophiâi Aigyptiôn,** 'in all the wisdom of the Egyptians'; and Rom. 11.26, **pâs Israêl,** 'all Israel'.

[22] 'You are being built up together', **synoikodomeisthe,** which Calvin took as imperative, i.e. '*be* built up together'.

The word for 'dwelling place', **katoikêtêrion,** only occurs here and in Rev. 18.2 in the NT but is common in the Septuagint. Paul may be referring to Ps. 76. 2 (AV), 'In Salem also is his tabernacle, and his dwelling place in Zion'. The Sept. version is even more appropriate to the theme of this passage: 'And his place was made *in peace* (**en eirênêi**), and his *dwelling place* (**katoikêtêrion**) in Sion.' **Eirênê** is the Greek for *shalom*. The identification of the name 'Salem' with 'peace' is seen also in Heb. 7.2.

'In the spirit' could mean 'by the aid of the Holy Spirit', but it is likely that it is a deliberate contrast with the unstated 'in the flesh'. In other words, the new Temple of God is a spiritual one, as distinct from the earthly Temple in Jerusalem, the 'temple made by hands' of Mark 14.58. Chrysostom certainly appears to favour this interpretation, since he explains the expression 'dwelling place in the spirit' as 'a spiritual house'.

# Chapter 3

1 For this reason, I, Paul, the prisoner of Christ Jesus for the sake of you Gentiles – 2 if, indeed, you have heard of the dispensation of the grace of God which was given to me [for ministering] to you, 3 that the secret was made known to me by way of a revelation, as I previously wrote in brief, 4 and in regard to this, if you read it, you can perceive my understanding of the secret of Christ,

[1] There is no verb in this verse, which is interrupted and not resumed until v. 14. We must take vv. 2–13 as being in parenthesis. This abrupt transition is typical of Paul's style especially when he is emotionally involved. See, for example, Gal. 2.3–10.

'Prisoner of Christ Jesus' is an oblique way of saying that although in the obvious sense he is the prisoner of the Roman emperor, he is really the prisoner of Christ because Christ is the real Lord and had ordained that this should happen. Incidentally, 'Jesus' is omitted in some manuscripts.

'For the sake of you Gentiles', because he had been imprisoned directly as a result of his ministry to them. The original charge, which had led eventually to Paul being sent to Rome, was that he had polluted the Temple by bringing Gentiles into the place (Acts 21.28). Before this charge was made, his opponents had been accusing Paul of persuading Jews not to circumcise their children and to abandon the Law (Acts 21.21).

[2] 'If, indeed', **ei ge**, as in Col. 1.23. Some commentators try to translate **ei ge** here as 'seeing that', but this is not its accepted meaning. See the notes on Col. 1.23.

'The dispensation', **oikonomiân**, i.e. the way God runs his household. See note on 1.10. Paul is referring here to the special gift he had received from God of bringing the gospel to the Gentiles. In Col. 1.25 the **oikonomiâ** is a stewardship given to Paul by God; here it seems that the stewardship which God himself exercizes is passed on to Paul.

'[For ministering] to you', **eis hûmâs**, which I translate in Col. 1.25 as 'over you'.

[3] 'The secret', **to mystêrion,** is the hidden truth, which God has now revealed, of his wish to include the Gentiles in his plan of redemption. See the notes on Col. 1.26 regarding **mystêrion**.

'By way of a revelation', **kata apokalypsin**, refers most probably to the revelation by Ananias to Paul of God's plan for him (Acts 9.15–17), namely, that Paul was to preach to the Gentiles. This is more likely than the suggestion that it refers to Paul's vision of Christ on the Damascus road. See also in *Reading Through Galatians* my notes on the use of this phrase in Gal. 2.2.

'As I previously wrote' must refer to an earlier letter now lost, as Chrysostom, Jerome and other early commentators assumed, because he goes on in the next verse to ask them to read it. Some commentators, however, see this as referring to previous remarks in this letter regarding the special mission to the Gentiles, but it is difficult to see what he has said before in this letter on the matter, apart from his statement in 1.9 that God had made known 'to *us* the secret of his will'. It is clear that Paul is asking his recipients to look up an account of his conversion and the start of his mission to the Gentiles. These biographical details seem to have been a standard part of Paul's preaching, as we can see in Acts 22.3–16 and 26.4–18.

[4] 'My understanding of the secret', **tên synesin mou en tôi**

**mystêriôi**, literally, 'my comprehension in the secret', refers to Paul's special understanding of the fact that the Gentiles were part of the redemption procured by Christ. I have to record that some regard this statement as boastful and unworthy of Paul; hence, they argue, he could not have written it. Presumably the self-deprecating tone of v. 8, 'the very least of all the saints', is more acceptable.

5 which was not made known to the sons of men, to other generations, as it has now been revealed to his holy apostles and prophets in the Spirit, 6 that the Gentiles are joint heirs, belong to a joint body and are joint sharers in the promise in Christ Jesus through the gospel, 7 of which I was made a servant according to God's gift of grace given to me according to the working of his power.

[5] 'To other generations', **heterais geneais**, which could also be translated '*in* other generations'.

'Holy', as applied to the group to which Paul undoubtedly belonged, causes problems to some, again because they see this as an indication of the writer's arrogance. A moment's reflection, however, will remind us that all Christians are called 'holy' because they belong to the Lord and have been dedicated to him. Holiness in the NT is not the same as moral superiority.

'Prophets in the Spirit', **prophêtais en pneumati**, are those who prophesy by the Holy Spirit, such as Ananias, whose prophecies led to Paul undertaking his mission to the Gentiles. It is possible that 'in the Spirit' here is meant to contrast with 'in the flesh', **en sarki**, but it would be wrong to identify the prophets 'in the flesh' with any OT prophets, since they also were regarded as being inspired by God.

[6] This verse sums up the main theme of this chapter. The emphasis on 'joint', **syn-**, is clear from the use of the three

terms: 'joint heirs', **syngklêronoma**, 'belong to a joint body', **syssôma** (a word apparently coined by Paul), and 'joint sharers', **symmetocha**. The Vulg. has *coheredes et concorporales et conparticipes*, but the AV does not try to reproduce this repetition. See notes regarding **syn-** on 2.6 and 4.16, and Col. 1.17 and 2.12.

'The promise' is that given to Abraham. See the notes on 2.12.

[7] This verse recalls v. 2. Note the typically inelegant repetition of 'according to', **kata**. Again I have resisted the temptation to vary the translation for stylistic reasons.

'Working', **energeian**. See the note on Col.1.29.

8 This grace was given to me, the very least of all the saints, that I should tell the Gentiles the good news of the unfathomable treasures of Christ, 9 and enlighten everyone as to the nature of the dispensation of the secret hidden from the ages by God who created all things, 10 in order that the most subtle wisdom of God might be made known now to the rulers and authorities in the heavenly places through the church, 11 according to the eternal purpose which he realized in Christ Jesus our Lord, 12 in whom we have freedom of speech and a confident introduction through faith in him.

[8] 'Very least', **elachistoterôi**, an ungrammatical form of superlative, 'leastest' or, as the AV has it, 'less than the least'. Compare I Cor. 15.9, 'I am the *least* (**elachistos**) of the apostles, and am not fit to be called an apostle, because I persecuted God's church.' Some commentators think Paul is playfully alluding here to his diminutive size. Apart from such a remark being irrelevant and out of place in such a solemn passage, the

108      *Reading Through Ephesians*

Corinthians parallel shows that he is referring to his moral and not his physical stature.

'Tell . . . the good news', **euangelisasthai**. The AV 'preach' is rather austere.

[9] 'Dispensation', **oikonomiâ**. The AV has 'fellowship' because the text it is based on had **koinôniâ** instead of **oikonomiâ**. The AV also adds 'by Jesus Christ' after 'all things', again because the text is different.

'From the ages', **apo tôn aiônôn**, is translated by some as 'since the beginning' or 'for ages past', but it must refer to the previous ages or eras of human history, from which the 'secret', **mystêriou**, has been hidden. In Col. 1.26 'from the ages' is coupled with 'from the generations'.

[10] 'The most subtle wisdom', **hê polypoikilos sophiâ**, Vulg. *multiformis sapientia*, does not convey the richness and beauty of objects described as **polypoikilos**, a word found nowhere else in the NT, and which was used to describe intricate and gorgeous wreaths and garments.

Who are 'the rulers and authorities in the heavenly places'? Thompson assumes they 'stand for all the forces that try to wreck and undermine human existence', but there is no need to assume they are all evil, although where 'the rulers and authorities' appear again in 6.12, they most certainly are. Most probably they include the angels, who, despite being in the presence of God, did not know his plan for human redemption before he revealed it to the world. The notion that the angels do not know what God intends is found in I Peter 1.12, 'matters which the angels want to peer into'. Note that this knowledge is mediated to them 'through the church', **dia tês ekklêsiâs**.

[11] 'Eternal purpose', **prothesin tôn aiônôn**, literally, 'purpose of the ages'.

'Realized', **epoiêsen**, literally, 'made'.

[12] 'Freedom of speech', **parrhêsiân**, is preferable here to 'boldness' (AV). See my notes on Heb. 3.6 in *Reading Through Hebrews*.

'Confident introduction', **prosagôgên en pepoithêsei**. The literal translation, 'introduction in confidence', would denote something entirely different, i.e. a private audience.

'Through faith in him', **dia tês pisteôs autou**, not 'through his faith'. For a discussion of this use of **pistis** with an objective genitive, see in *Reading Through Galatians* the notes on Gal. 2.16.


13 Therefore, I beseech that you do not lose heart at my sufferings on your behalf – they are your glory. 14 For this reason, I bend my knees before the Father, 15 after whom all fatherhood in heaven and earth is named,


[13] 'That *you* do not lose heart', as AV 'that *ye* faint not', and Vulg. *ne deficiatis*, i.e. 'you', is better than 'that *I* do not lose heart'. Paul is saying that they should not be demoralized, but rather feel proud that he is suffering for them.

[14] 'For this reason' picks up from 'for this reason' in v. 1, and now, after the long digression, we have the main verb, 'I bend'. Several manuscripts add 'of our Lord Jesus Christ' after 'Father', but the best ones omit the phrase.

[15] 'All fatherhood', **pâsa patriâ**, Vulg. *omnis paternitas*, appears in most modern translations as 'family'. This is due to the influence of the AV, which followed the Geneva version in translating the phrase as 'the whole family'. Tyndale, however, wished to bring out the connection between 'Father' in the previous verse and 'fatherhood' here, and translated this verse 'which is father over all that is called father in heaven and earth'. This was also the translation favoured by Cranmer. The

word 'family' obviously cannot be *named* (**onomazetai**) after 'Father', since we require a word which is etymologically connected with 'father'. Hence 'lineage', i.e. descent on the male line, which would be better translation of **patriâ** than 'family', is also to be rejected. Paul is making the Platonist point that all examples of 'fatherliness' are mere copies of the ideal 'Father' in heaven. All early scholars saw this point. Athanasius (*Against the Arians*, 1.23) says, 'For God does not imitate man, but rather men [imitate] God, because he is properly and alone truly Father of his own Son, and *they have been named* (**ônomasthêsan**) as fathers of their own children themselves.' Theodoret also says that God 'is truly Father, and he does not have this [name] because he has taken it from someone else, but rather has allowed the others to share it'.

Examples of fatherhood 'on earth' are easy to find, but what examples could there be 'in heaven' other that the Father himself? Theodoret suggested that there are two types of father, bodily (**sômatikoi**) and spiritual (**pneumatikoi**). 'He calls the spiritual ones the 'heavenly' ones; such was the divine Apostle himself.' We should not, however, interpret this verse as though it is saying that there are other fathers in heaven than the Father himself. Paul is simply saying that all fathers, wherever they are, are copies of the Father.

16 that, according to the richness of his glory, he may grant that you be strengthened in the core of your personality with power through his Spirit, 17 that Christ dwell in your hearts through faith, [that you be] rooted and grounded in love, 18 that you may have power to comprehend with all the saints what [is] the breadth, length, height and depth [of it], 19 and to know the love of Christ that surpasses understanding, so that you may be filled with all the fullness of God.

[16] 'Richness of his glory', **to ploutos tês doxês autou**, a

phrase also found in Rom. 9.23. See 1.18 and Col. 1.27 for extensions of this phrase.

'In the core of your personality', **eis ton esô anthrôpon**, literally, 'in the inner man'.

[17] 'Rooted and grounded' (a marvellous mixed metaphor like that in Col. 2.7), **errhizômenoi kai tethemeliômenoi**, grammatically speaking, should be genitive, agreeing with 'your', i.e. 'of you', not nominative. Hence it is best to assume that the verb 'be' has been omitted and that this is another clause introduced by **hina**, 'that'. The alternative solution, which violates the normal word order, is to take the two participles with the next clause. In other words, the next verse would start 'that, *being rooted and grounded in love*, you may have power . . . etc.'

[18] I have added '[of it]', but this begs the question; 'the breadth, length, height and depth' of *what*? Many suggestions have been put forward, some of them fanciful. For instance, Origen, who was very fond of allegory, saw it as a reference to the cross, by which Jesus ascended on *high*, descended to the *depths*, and has now reached over the *breadth* and *length* of the earth. Gregory of Nyssa adapted this idea, seeing the portion above the crossbeam as the height, the lower section as the depth and the two arms as the length and breadth. Jerome saw the height as a reference to the good angels, the depth as the wicked ones, the length as denoting those human beings striving to reach heaven and the breadth as those on the way to destruction. It has even been suggested that the passage refers to the dimensions of the temple or church of Christ. As Calvin said, 'These please through their subtlety; but what have they to do with Paul's thinking?' Chrysostom thought that it referred to the 'dispensation of the secret' of v. 9. Most commentators, however, suggest more plausibly that it refers to the 'love' of vv. 17 and 19.

[19] The paradox of this verse, i.e. to know what is beyond knowledge, is deliberate. Luther thought that 'surpasses' meant 'was better than'. In other words, to love Christ is better than knowledge. Our writer, however, seems to be recalling here the 'unfathomable treasures of Christ' of v. 8 by referring to a love which is so vast that it is beyond our understanding. This notion of a power beyond our comprehension continues in the next verse.

'The fullness', **to plêrôma**, is what fills up our emptiness. It includes the grace, virtue and power of God and all those good things which he has promised to us as his children, such as eternal life and joy. It is, of course, impossible to define. See my notes on Col.1.19 and Eph.1.23.

20 To him who can do far more and beyond all that we can ask or think, according to the power which operates within us, 21 to him [be] glory in the church and in Christ Jesus to all the generations of the age of ages, amen.

[20] 'Far more' is an inadequate translation of **hyperekperis-sou**, Vulg. *superabundanter*. Paul is very fond of **hyper**-compounds, and this is one that he uses also in I Thess. 3.10 and 5.13. Its literal sense is 'beyond what is more than sufficient'.

The meaning of this verse is not easy to follow, but Paul seems to be saying that God can do more than we ask because he has enabled *us* to do more than we ask. The miracles we perform are the miracles he performs due to his power which is working in us.

[21] 'In the church and in Christ Jesus' differs from the AV 'in the church by Christ Jesus', because the text on which the AV was based did not contain 'and'.

'To all the generations of the age of ages' is a conflation of 'to all generations' and 'to the age of ages', i.e. 'for ever and ever'. There are several variants of the latter expression in the NT. We find **eis tous aiônas tôn aiônôn**, 'into the ages of the ages', but we can also have **eis ton aiôna tou aiônos**, 'into the age of the age', or the shorter forms **eis ton aiôna** and **eis tous aiônas**.

# Chapter 4

1 So I beseech you, I, the prisoner in the Lord, to walk in a way worthy of the calling you have received, 2 with all modesty and gentleness and with patience tolerating one another in love, 3 diligent to preserve the unity of the Spirit by the bond of peace.

[1] 'Prisoner in the Lord' has two meanings: he is the prisoner *of* the Lord (see notes on 3.1), and he is in, or with, the Lord despite being a prisoner.

'In a way worthy', **axiôs**, i.e. 'worthily', is only used by Paul in the NT, apart from one occurrence in III John 6.

[2] 'Modesty', or 'humility', **tapeinophrosynês**, in Col. 2.18 is translated as 'fasting'. See the notes on Col. 3.12 which refer to 'modesty, gentleness and patience'.

'Tolerating', **anechomenoi**, occurs in Col. 3.13.

[3] 'The unity of the Spirit' is picked up by 'one Spirit' in the next verse.

'*By* the bond of peace', **en tôi syndesmôi tês eirênês**, rather than '*in* the bond of peace', because peace is the means by which unity is preserved. See the notes on Col. 3.14.

4 One body and one Spirit, just as you were called in one hope of your calling; 5 one Lord, one faith, one

baptism, 6 one God and Father of all, who is over all and through all and in all.

[4–6] The key to this passage seems to be v. 5. It has been observed that in Greek the word for 'one' occurs in all three gender forms: 'one Lord', **heis** (masculine) **Kûrios**; 'one faith', **mia** (feminine) **pistis**; 'one baptism', **hen** (neuter) **baptisma**. The Vulgate reproduces the same phenomenon: *unus dominus, una fides, unum baptisma.* Could this be a triad taught to new Christians to help them to remember basic doctrine, a catechist's formula? If we arrange all the nouns in these verses according to gender we find other triads emerging:

| Heis | | Mia | | Hen | |
|------|------|------|------|------|------|
| **Kûrios** | Lord | **pistis** | faith | **baptisma** | baptism |
| **Patêr** | Father | **klêsis** | calling | **pneuma** | Spirit |
| **theos** | God | **elpis** | hope | **sôma** | body |

It would not be difficult to construct a specific doctrinal connection between the nouns on each line. For example, 'the Father calls us in one Spirit', or 'God is the hope of the body of the church'. We can, of course, rearrange the nouns so that they form different combinations. It seems more than coincidence that all the nouns in this passage are accounted for, that there are exactly three of each gender, and that the word 'one' occurs seven times. It would be asking too much to expect 'one' to occur nine times. Do we have echoes of similar connections elsewhere? For example, does I Cor. 10.17, 'one bread, one body', **heis artos, hen sôma** (masculine and neuter respectively), come from another triad, a triad which included the words 'one fellowship', **mia koinôniâ** (feminine), a word which is used in the previous verse? And again, is it just a coincidence that in I John 5.7, 8, the 'three that bear witness', i.e. the spirit, **pneuma;** the water, **hydôr;** and the blood, **haima** are all neuter nouns, and that Paul's favourite triad, 'faith, hope and love', are all feminine?

'Over all', clearly because he is the supreme Lord. Perhaps 'through all', because he acts through all, and 'in all', because he is omnipresent. It is not possible to know whether Paul is referring to human beings, i.e. 'all men', or creation itself, i.e. 'all things', since the words for 'all' occur in forms that could be either masuline or neuter. The Vulg. has *super omnes et per omnia et in omnibus nobis*, which assumes the first and third are masculine and the second neuter. Note, however, that the Vulgate is based on a text which added 'us', **hêmîn**, at the end of the verse. The AV's 'in you all' is based on a text which added **humîn**, 'you'.

**7 To each one of us grace has been given according to the measure of the gift of Christ. 8 Therefore he says, 'When he ascended on high, he took prisoners captive, gave gifts to human kind.' 9 And what does this 'he ascended' mean, if not that he also descended into the lower parts of the earth?**

[7] In short, Christ has given each one different gifts.

[8] 'He says', i.e. God speaking through scripture. Quotations from the Psalms are sometimes attributed to David, but note Heb. 4.7, 'speaking in [the psalm of] David', and Acts 4.25, 'having spoken by the mouth of your servant David'. This quotation is from Ps. 68.18, with some variations from the Septuagint version, which goes, 'You have ascended into the height, you have made captive captivity, you have taken gifts among men.' The AV has '*for* men', but is otherwise basically the same. The most notable variations in Paul's version are 'gave' and '*to* men', for the Sept. 'taken' and '*among* men'. Most early commentators, such as Chrysostom, argued that the meaning was substantially the same. Theophylact, for instance, said, 'for God, giving the gifts, receives in return the service', but it looks as though Paul was quoting from a

different text. The Aramaic version, known as a Targum, has 'gave to men', and it is likely that this is the version Paul was using.

'Took prisoners captive', i.e. captured a body of men and made them captives, is more comprehensible than the usual 'made (or led) captivity captive'. Who are the captives? Chrysostom thought they were 'the enemies of Christ, Satan, sin and death'. Theodoret thought that they were the redeemed, who were prisoners of Satan when Christ captured them. Both interpretations could be correct, as Hodge suggests in his commentary: 'Christ has conquered Satan and leads him captive, and it is also true that he redeems his people and subdues them to himself and leads them as willing captives.'

[9] The argument of this verse is that Christ's ascension to heaven was necessarily linked with his descent into Hades. 'Into the lower parts of the earth', **eis ta katôtera merê tês gês**, refers to the parts beneath the earth and, as Chrysostom, Theophylact and Theodoret all say, stands for death. Many of the early commentators use the word 'Hades', but that is substantially the same thing. Some modern commentators try to interpret the phrase to mean the earth, i.e. the 'lower parts' *are* the earth which lies beneath the heavens, and they take this verse as a reference to the Incarnation of Christ. The NEB has 'to the lowest level, down to the very earth', but adds in a footnote, 'to the regions beneath the earth'. It is clear that the Greek phrase corresponds to the Hebrew *eretz tachtit*, 'the parts beneath the earth', and can never denote the surface of the earth. Compare Rom. 10.6–7, 'Do not say in your heart, "Who will ascend to heaven?", that is, bring Christ down, or, "Who will descend into the abyss?", that is, bring Christ up from the dead?' Heb. 2.7, 9, when speaking of Jesus being made lower than the angels, refers to his death, not his incarnation. I cannot find a single example of the phrase 'into the lower parts of the earth', or anything resembling it, used in reference to the incarnation. The standard phrase used in that

connection, as I note in reference to 2.17, is 'into the world', **eis ton kosmon**. It is also clear that in this passage Paul is referring to the death and subsequent ascension of Christ because he sees the two extremes as in some way completing the whole of the divine plan of redemption, from top to bottom, as it were.

10 The one who descended is the same one who ascended above all the heavens in order to fill all things. 11 And he himself gave some as apostles, some as prophets, some as evangelists, and some as shepherds and teachers, 12 with a view to the preparation of the saints, for the work of service, for the building up of the body of Christ, 13 until we all come to unity of faith and of the knowledge of the son of God, into a perfect man, into the measure of the maturity of the fullness of Christ,

[10] 'Fill', as we have already seen in 1.23, is a complex word. Christ *fills* everywhere with his presence, *fufils* all the prophecies of scripture, *completes* the whole plan of salvation, *accomplishes* all that is necessary and *perfects* all his servants with the gifts of grace.

[11] 'Gave', rather than 'appointed', because the verb **edôken** refers back to the **edôken** of v. 8. The apostles, prophets, etc. are Christ's gifts to the church.

'Some as shepherds and teachers', as Jerome points out, is not the same as 'some as shepherds and some as teachers'. In other words, the shepherds also have to be teachers. This, however, does not mean that no one is allowed simply to be a teacher – all shepherds are teachers, but not all teachers are shepherds. At this early stage in the development of the ministry in the church it is difficult to identify the precise duties and functions of the people mentioned in this verse. Theophylact took the 'shepherds' to be bishops and presbyters, and the 'teachers' to be deacons. Some of the commentaries listed at the back of this guide deal with the subject in more detail.

[12] Note the comma after saints. I take all the clauses as co-ordinate. In other words, the saints are not being prepared for the work of service, but the apostles, prophets, evangelists, shepherds and teachers have the job of preparing the saints, of serving, and of building up the body of Christ. When Chrysostom observes 'each one builds, each one prepares, each one serves', he is presumably speaking of the ministers mentioned in the previous verse.

[13] 'Into a perfect man', **eis andra teleion**, is a subtle phrase. Note firstly **eis**, 'into', not just 'to', and secondly **andra**, the word for a male, not **anthrôpon**, the generic term for a human being. This clearly refers to Christ, and is a more complex idea than that of the **kainos** or **neos anthrôpos**, 'the new man', of 2.15 and 4.24, and Col. 3.10, where the generic term for human being refers to the the new type of person the Christian becomes by being in Christ. Here we have a more complex and profound concept: our goal is not simply to become a better person, nor is it even just to come into the presence of the perfect man Christ, but actually to turn into him, to become the perfect man. This verse must be taken along with vv. 15 and 16 as part of Paul's vision of the church as the body of Christ. If the individual members are part of his body, they are, in effect, Christ himself. It is clear that the phrase 'grow into him' in v. 15 is referring back to the phrase 'into a perfect man'.

'Into the measure of the maturity of the fullness', **eis metron hêlikiâs tou plêrômatos,** defines the epithet 'perfect', **teleion.** In other words, the perfect man is fully grown or mature, complete and fulfilled. 'Maturity' is a better translation of **hêlikiâs** than the NEB's 'stature', which refers mainly to physical height. The Vulg. *aetatis*, i.e. 'age', is closer to the original.

14 so that we should no longer be infants, tossed around and made dizzy by every wind of doctrine, by the trickery of human beings, by villainy associated with the craftiness of deceit, 15 but, being truthful in love, let us in all respects grow into him, who is the head, Christ. 16 From him the whole body, being fitted and put together, via every joint through which it is supplied, according to the measured operation of each and every part, receives its increase and builds itself up in love.

[14] 'So that we should no longer . . .', i.e. 'Therefore we should no longer . . .'

'Infants', **nêpioi**, or 'childish', 'silly', contrasting with the mature adults of the previous verse.

'Tossed around', **klydônizomenoi**, is a nautical metaphor, as we can see from the use of the phrase 'wind of doctrine'. The verb is formed from the noun **klydôn**, 'billow', 'surf'.

'Made dizzy', **peripheromenoi**, literally, 'being carried around'. This verb is used in the Septuagint (Eccles.7.7) in the sense 'to make mad'.

'Trickery', **kybeiâi**, literally, 'dice-playing'; from **kybos**, 'a dice'.

There is no evidence for the suggestion that this verse is referring to the infiltration of a Gnostic type of heresy. It is possible that Paul is concerned about a Judaizing element in the church, as is clear throughout the letter to the Colossians, but the language used here makes it likely that he sees the danger as coming from a movement back to pagan practices.

[15] 'Being truthful' is picked up in v. 25, 'put off falsehood and speak truth – each with his neighbour', the reason being that 'we are the limbs of one another'. 'In love' here is the equivalent of this reason; in other words, 'because we love one another'.

[16] This complicated passage is easier to understand if we compare it with the parallel metaphor in Col. 2.19.

'Via every joint through which it is supplied', literally, 'through every joint of supply', **dia pâsês haphês tês epichorêgiâs,** clearly corresponds to the two expressions which appear in the Colossians passage, 'through its joints', **dia tôn haphôn,** and 'being supplied', **epichorêgoumenon.** We also have in both passages the participle '[being] put together', **symbibazomenon.** The Ephesians version of this metaphor is more elaborate, since the two clauses beginning with 'according to . . .' and 'builds itself up . . .' and the participle **synarmologoumenon,** 'being fitted [together]', have no equivalent in Colossians. The latter verb, incidentally, may have been coined by Paul (like the word **syssôma** in 3.6), since it is only found here and in 2.21, where it is used in a different metaphor, i.e. the building of the new Temple of God. It is significant that both of these new words incorporate the prefix **syn-,** 'together with', the key theme of the letter. The repeated use of this prefix throws an emphasis on the new unity individuals enjoy by their incorporation in the church.

The difference between the Colossians and Ephesians versions is significant since the additional material embodies doctrine which is the theme of this particular chapter, as we can see when we look back to verses 7 and 11–13. 'According to the measured operation (literally, 'according to the working in measure', **kat'energeian en metrôi**) of each and every part' and 'builds itself up in love' underline the fact that, while each member individually grows and has its own individual function to perform, this function is to be exercised in harmony with the other members. In short, there has to be unity in diversity.

Some commentators translate the phrase 'via every joint' as '*by* every joint' and take it with the preceding verbs. For example, the NEB has 'bonded and knit together *by* every constituent joint'. But it is clear that it is the head, i.e. Christ, which holds the body together. Similarly, it is the head, not the joints, which supplies the body's needs. The joints pass on what the head supplies; they are not the original suppliers. This is more obvious in the Colossians version of this metaphor. Note also the use of present participles, '*being* fitted together', '*being* put together', which indicate that it is a continuing process, not a completed state. This is not apparent in the NEB 'bonded and knit together'.

17 So I say this, and I declare in the Lord, that you should no longer live like the Gentiles live in the emptiness of their minds, 18 with their understanding darkened and excluded from the life of God through the ignorance that exists in them, due to the hardness of their hearts, 19 since, in becoming brutalized, they have abandoned themselves to outrageous behaviour, to practise every kind of filthiness in excess.

[17] 'I declare', **martûromai**, i.e. 'I make a solemn statement'. See the notes on the use of this verb in Gal. 5.3 in *Reading Through Galatians*.

'Live', literally, 'walk'. This metaphor, which occurs in seven verses in this letter, is also common in other letters.

'Emptiness', **mataiotêti**, also 'vanity', 'purposelessness', 'foolishness'.

[18] 'Darkened', **eskotômenoi**, contrasts with the light of the Christian believer, which is referred to in the next chapter.

'Excluded', **apêllotriômenoi**. See note on Col. 1.21.

'Life of God', i.e. eternal life, rather than just a life lived in accordance with God or, as Theodoret puts it, 'the life [lived] in virtue'. **Zôê**, the word used here, is more than **bios**, which often has the meaning 'way of life'. The verb **zaô**, as we can see in many passages in the NT, means 'to be alive', rather than 'to live one's life'.

'Hardness', **pôrôsin**, is the medical word for a 'callus', the hard skin that forms over an area that has been rubbed. There is no evidence that the word means 'blindness', although we can see that the insensitivity caused by a callus could metaphorically be described as such.

[19] 'Brutalized', **apêlgêkotes**, literally 'having put away pain' or 'being past feeling'. This continues the callus metaphor of the previous verse, as Theodoret correctly explains, 'for calluses that occur on the body have no feeling'. Hardness leads to insensitivity, then lack of feeling.

'Outrageous behaviour', **aselgeiâi**, covers a wide range of anti-social activities from hooliganism to lewdness. It does not necessarily denote sexual misbehaviour.

'Filthiness', **akatharsiâs**.

'Excess', **pleonexiâi**, literally, 'trying to have more (than one should)'. The NEB 'stop at nothing to satisfy their foul desires' is a reasonable translation of the last clause of this verse. See the notes on Col. 3.5 regarding **akatharsiâ** and **pleonexiâ**.

20 But this is not how you understood Christ, 21 if, indeed, you did hear him and were taught by him, according to what is true in Jesus, 22 that you should put off the old man of your former life, who perishes in the pursuit of his deceitful desires, 23 and be renewed in the spirit of your mind, 24 and put on the new man who was created in accordance with God in the righteousness and holiness of truth.

[20] 'Understood', or 'learned', **emathete**.

[21] 'If, indeed', **ei ge**. See note on Col. 1.23.

'According to what is true in Jesus', literally '*as* (**kathôs**) is truth in Jesus'. This does not mean '*since* the truth is in Jesus'. Abbott paraphrases it correctly: 'as is right teaching in Jesus'.

[22] 'Old man', **palaion anthrôpon**: see notes on v.13.

'Of your former life', **kata tên proterân anastrophên**, literally, 'according to the former way of life', AV 'concerning the former conversation'.

'Who perishes', **phtheiromenon**, literally, 'being destroyed'.

[23] An alternative translation would be 'and be spiritually renewed in your minds'.

[24] The 'new man', a term which occurs also in Col. 3.10, is the 'new creation' of II Cor. 5.17 and Gal. 6.15, and refers to the new state of the believer in Christ.

'In accordance with God', **kata Theon**, not 'after the likeness of God' but 'according to God's will'.

'In the righteousness and holiness of truth' could also be 'in true righteousness and holiness' or 'in righteousness and true holiness' (AV).

25 Therefore put off falsehood and 'speak truth – each with his neighbour', because we are the limbs of one another. 26 'Be angry and sin not'; let the sun not set on your anger; 27 do not give the devil room. 28 Let him who steals, steal no longer, but rather let him toil hard with his own hands in some good work in order to have something to share with anyone in need.

[25] The quotation is from Zech. 8.16.

[26] This quotation is from the Sept. version of Ps. 4.4, (AV) '*Stand in awe* and sin not'. The reason for the discrepancy is that the Hebrew original translated in the AV as 'stand in awe' actually means 'tremble'. One can tremble with fear or anger, and in other OT passages it is sometimes translated as 'be angry'.

'Let the sun not set on your anger' means that you should not let your anger fester. Anger is sometimes justified, but, if you allow it to linger, you give the devil an opportunity of using it for evil purposes.

[27] 'Room', **topon**, means literally 'place', hence 'opportunity'. Some commentators, such as Luther and Erasmus, took the word translated here as 'devil', **diabolôi**, in its original sense of 'accuser', and so the sentence could be interpreted as either a condemnation of those in the church who brought accusations against fellow Christians or a warning to Christians not to do anything which would give outsiders an opportunity to accuse them. The word **diabolos**, however, in the NT usually refers to Satan. Paul generally uses 'Satan', **Satanâs**, but **diabolos** is a common word for the devil in the Gospels, apart from Mark. It occurs in both of the letters to Timothy.

[28] This verse is not simply referring to the crime of stealing or robbery; as Jerome rightly observes, it covers any activity which causes someone else to suffer a loss, any dishonest trade, in fact. The clue is to be found in the Talmudic saying, 'One who does not teach his son an occupation, teaches him to be a brigand.'

'Toil hard', **kopiâtô**, literally, 'tire oneself out', as in Col. 1.29.

29 May no unsound word come out of your mouth, but [only] what is good for the improvement of the occasion, to give some benefit to those who hear it. 30 And do not grieve the Holy Spirit of God, by whom you have been sealed until the day of redemption. 31 Let all bitterness, anger, bad temper, shouting and abuse, be removed from you, along with all maliciousness. 32 And be kind to one another, tender-hearted, forgiving one another, just as God in Christ forgave you.

[29] 'Unsound', **sapros**, i.e. 'rotten', 'diseased'.

'For the improvement of the occasion', **pros oikodomên tês chreiâs**, literally, 'in regard to building of need', hence the Vulg. *ad aedificationem opportunitatis*. The AV 'to the use of edifying' is inaccurate. **Chreiâ** is 'need', hence 'what the situation asks for'. Perhaps 'to meet the need' might be a reasonable translation of this phrase. Jerome observed that there was an alternative reading of *fidei*, 'of faith', in some Latin manuscripts. This is based on a reading in the original Greek of **pisteôs** for **chreiâs**, but it is not found in the best manuscripts.

'Benefit', **charin**, a word which I discuss in the note on Col. 4.6, the parallel passage to this, can also mean 'grace', 'joy', 'pleasure', 'charm' or 'gratitude'. Hence Chrysostom gives two definitions: 'either so that the hearer[s] should be grateful to you, or so that you should cause them to be full of grace (or 'favoured', **kecharitômenous**).' See also my notes on 1.6; Col. 3.16; and on Gal. 1.3 in *Reading through Galatians*.

[30] 'You have been sealed', **esphrâgisthête**, i.e. 'marked with a seal'. This applied to items specially marked for consignment or set apart for the owner. It could mean 'you have been approved', but this is a secondary meaning of the verb, and much rarer. The commercial metaphor is continued with the phrase 'until the day of redemption', **eis hêmerân apolytrôseôs**, that is, either 'the day when you will receive the full payment of your inheritance', as in 1.14, or, more likely in this context, 'the day when you will be finally set free'.

[31] The terms used in this verse, which recalls Col. 3.8, have been more methodically arranged in a scale ranging from 'bitterness', **pikriâ**, the initial resentment; through 'anger', **thûmos**, i.e. the first outburst of anger; then 'bad temper', **orgê**, where one has been taken over by more permanent feelings of anger; then 'shouting', **kraugê**, the loud expression of anger; to the final stage of 'abuse', **blasphêmiâ**, the direction of resent-

ment against another individual. The last also covers 'slander' or 'defamation' They are all summed up under the heading of 'maliciousness' or 'malice', **kakiâ**. The Vulgate translates these vices as *amaritudo, ira, indignatio, clamor, blasphemia*, and *malitia*.

[32] This verse and v.2 taken together correspond to Col. 3.12, 13.

'Forgiving', **charizomenoi**. The verb **charizomai** can have as many meanings as the noun **charis**. See above note on v. 29.

# Chapter 5

1 So be imitators of God as children whom he loves, 2 and live your lives in love, as Christ also loved us and gave himself for us as an offering and sacrifice to God for a sweet-smelling savour. 3 But fornication and all filthiness or excess should not even be named amongst you, as is right for holy people, 4 together with shameful behaviour, and stupid talk or ribaldry, things which would not be fitting, but rather [there should be] giving of thanks.

[1–4] These verses should be taken in the context of the following verses, which are to do with the behaviour of pagans at their festivals and social gatherings. The moral failings identified here are associated with their behaviour on such occasions.

[2] 'Us' is a better reading than 'you', which is found in some manuscripts. The confusion between 'us', hêmâs, and 'you', hûmâs, is probably due to the fact that at a later period they became indistinguishable in pronunciation.

Chrysostom says, 'Can you see that suffering on behalf of an enemy is a sweet-smelling savour and an acceptable sacrifice? And if you are killed, then you will be a sacrifice; that is to imitate God.' The implication behind this verse is that, while it is a convincing expression of love to die for one's friends, to die for one's enemies, as Christ did, is the most sublime act of love.

[3] For 'fornication', 'filthiness' and 'excess' see the notes on Col. 3.5. NEB's 'ruthless greed' is not correct in this context, which clearly is one of sexual immorality.

'*Should not even be named* ( **mêde onomazesthô**) amongst you', in other words, no one should be able to identify them as vices which exist amongst you. It does not mean, 'should not even be *mentioned by you*'. Paul is concerned with the reputation of Christians in the eyes of their pagan acquaintances. He is obviously not saying that the names of such vices cannot be spoken; after all, he is mentioning them himself. A similar expression occurs in I Cor. 5. 11, 'But now I have written to you not to mix with any brother *who is named* (**onomazomenos**) as a fornicator, or as *someone indulging to excess* (**pleonektês**), or as an idolater, as abusive, as a drunkard, or as an extortioner.'

[4] 'Shameful behaviour', **aischrotês**, is often used by classical writers to denote forms of sexual deviancy.

'Stupid talk', **môrologiâ**, is plainly more than making silly remarks.

'Ribaldry', **eutrapeliâ**, a term which usually means 'witty repartee'. Here it obviously denotes coarse jesting. Note that this verse is the only passage in the the NT where these three nouns are found. It is another noun that we find defined in Aristotle (*Nicomachean Ethics*, 1108a, 24), but not in the bad sense which it has here. This is probably because Paul regarded the occasion when witty repartee was customary, i.e. a pagan religious festival, as itself morally suspect.

'Things which would not be fitting', **ha ouk anêken**: see the note on Col. 3.18 regarding this conditional sense of the imperfect tense common with verbs of obligation.

'Giving thanks', **eucharistiâ**, a word used fifteen times in the NT, did not at this early period refer to the eucharist. It seems odd to suggest that the Christian response in situations where everybody is indulging in coarse or obscene conversation should be to offer thanks, hence some early scholars suggested that the word meant 'gracious speech'. However, the word always means 'thanksgiving' in the NT. Paul seems to be saying that a Christian, like any Jew in a similar situation, in the company of those celebrating a festival in honour of some pagan deity, should turn to God, i.e. pray, offering praise and thanks instead to the Creator.

5 For this you know and perceive, that every fornicator or impure person or anyone who indulges to excess, that is, an idolater, has no inheritance in the kingdom of Christ and of God. 6 Let no one deceive you with empty words; for it is because of these things that the wrath of God is visited on the children of disobedience. 7 So do not be partakers with them.

[5] 'Anyone who indulges to excess', **pleonektês**; compare **pleonexiâ**, 'excess', in 4.19, Col. 3.5, and v. 3 of this chapter.

'That is, an idolator', **ho estin eidôlolatrês**, is preferable to the AV reading 'who is an idolater', **hos estin eidôlolatrês**, found in a few manuscripts. The Vulgate has *idolorum servitus*, 'idolatry', which must be based on a manuscript which had **eidôlolatriâ**, probably due to confusion with Col. 3.5, instead of **eidôlolatrês**. Incidentally, the NEB paraphrase, 'the greed which makes an idol of gain', is incorrect on two counts, not only because it treats the reference to idolatry as metaphorical, but also because it mistranslates **pleonektês**. See the notes on Col. 3.5.

'Of Christ and of God', i.e. 'of the Son and of the Father', not 'of Christ, who is God'. The kingdom of God is also Christ's kingdom.

[6] What are the 'empty words'? Probably, the argument that there is nothing wrong in taking part in pagan festivities, provided that you do not actually worship the gods being celebrated.

[7] 'Partakers with them', i.e. sharing in their festivities.

8 For you were once darkness but now [you are] light in the Lord; behave like children of light 9 – for the fruit of light [is seen] in every [form of] goodness, righteousness and truth – 10 testing what is well-pleasing to the Lord, 11 and do not share with [them] in the barren works of darkness, but rather actually refute them. 12 For it is shameful even to speak of the things done by them in secret.

[8] Thompson thinks that the 'darkness' meant for the Jews 'being out of touch with the will and purpose of God and being in the power of forces opposed to him'. This may be so, but Paul is clearly addressing people who were pagans, not Jews, before they were converted to Christianity. See the notes on Col. 1.12 regarding the significance of 'light'.

'Children of light': see I Thess. 5.5.

[9] 'Fruit of light' is similar to the 'fruit of the spirit' of Gal. 5.22 (where it is contrasted with the 'works of the flesh' of v.19), and the 'fruit of righteousness' of Phil. 1.11. AV has 'of the Spirit', since the text used by the translators had **pneumatos**, instead of 'of the light', **phôtos**. The best manuscripts, however, have the latter. The variation probably arose from a scribe conforming with the reading in Galatians.

[10] 'Testing', **dokimazontes**, can mean 'approving', but in the majority of cases this verb, which is a favourite word of Paul, seems to have the sense of 'prove for oneself', 'examine', 'scrutinize', hence 'test'. In I Thess. 2.4 it would appear to mean 'examine and approve', but elsewhere in the same letter (5.21) 'test' is clearly a better translation. 'To approve' is a secondary meaning; the basic meaning is 'to test'.

[11] 'Share', **syngkoinôneite**, a verb which means 'to take part in something along with someone else', not just 'to take part'.

'Barren', **akarpois**, literally, 'fruit-less', picks up the reference to 'fruit', **karpos**, in v. 9.

'Refute', **elengcheté** (AV 'reprove'). This is not an easy verb to define since it has a wide range of meanings. It is frequently found in the sense 'cross-examine' or 'accuse'. It can also mean 'test', as in Heb. 12.5, but this cannot be the meaning here, since there is no need to test the 'works of darkness'; they are patently wicked. A closer meaning is 'expose', which seems to be the sense it has in John 3.20, 'For everyone who does evil hates the light and does not come to the light, lest his deeds *should be exposed* (**elengchthêi**)', but that should be rejected, too, since the same verb is used in v. 13, where translating **ta elengchomena** as 'things that are *exposed*' would produce a tautology. 'Expose', in fact, does not carry enough force. The meaning 'refute/confute', i.e. 'prove that they are false or wrong', conveys more of the strong tone of criticism.

'Actually', **kai**, or 'in fact', 'indeed'. Paul is saying in effect, 'Don't just avoid taking part in these activities; speak up – point out how wrong they are.'

[12] This verse should not be taken too literally. Although it is shameful to talk about these things, the Christian has to do so if he is to criticize them. The writer means to say that these activities are so bad that even talking about them is disgusting. Doing them is even worse.

13 All things that are refuted are revealed by the light.
14 For everything that is revealed is light. That is why it says,
'O sleeper, awake!
Arise from the dead,
And Christ will shine upon you.'

[13] 'Are revealed', **phaneroutai**, Vulg. *manifestantur*, AV 'are made manifest'.

[14] 'Everything that is revealed' (passive), **pân to phaner-oumenon**, not the AV 'whatsoever doth make manifest', i.e. 'everything that reveals' (active). Some commentators have had problems with this verse because of the paradox implicit in the statement that sinful things, when exposed to the light, actually become light. They prefer the easier, but bland, statement 'everything that reveals is light', even though it violates the rules of grammar. It is impossible for this verb to be treated as a middle (a verb that looks passive but is actually active), especially when it is clearly passive in the previous verse, as Hodge points out. The paradox is perhaps more acceptable if we apply it to sinners, who were formerly in a state of darkness, but when Christ's light shone upon them, they were illuminated; they became light itself. So sin disappears and becomes light.

'It says': what, or who, says? And where? Jerome could not trace this quotation, which is slightly reminiscent of Isa. 60.1 (AV), 'Arise, shine; for thy light is come, and the glory of the Lord is risen upon thee.' Most scholars believe that this is a fragment from a baptismal hymn; some have even recognized that it has a metrical pattern. Abbott, for instance, draws attention to 'its rhythmical character'. I believe that it is possible to identify the metre used in composing these lines. The Greek reads as follows:

> **egeire, ho katheudôn:**
> kai anastâ ek tôn nekrôn,
> kai epiphausei soi ho Christos.

Without going into all the technical details, which I hope to outline elsewhere, we can reconstruct the original to read:

> **egeiron, ô katheudôn:**
> ek tôn nekrôn anastâ,
> kai phôtisei se Christos.

I have substituted the verb **phôtisei** for **epiphausei**, since it is the verb frequently used in the context of baptism, and occurs in the Sept. version of the passage from Isaiah quoted above ('Shine, arise' is rendered **phôtizou, phôtizou**), and the verb **epiphauskô** does not occur in verse. We now have three standard Anacreontic lines based on the following pattern:

$$u - u - u - -$$
$$- - u - u - -$$
$$- - u - u - -$$

Anacreontics were associated in the classical world with drinking songs and light erotic verse, but they were used by such Christian writers as Gregory of Nazianzus and Synesius when writing on sacred subjects. In a passage where Paul is warning his audience about the dangers of taking part in the revelry associated with pagan celebration, it is appropriate that he should remind them of a better use for a good tune.

Why did Paul quote this hymn inaccurately? Perhaps he felt it was too sacred to quote publicly in its normal form, perhaps he was simply giving the gist of the hymn. After all, it is the theology behind it that was relevant to his argument. We cannot know the reason, but it it is fascinating to think that this could be the earliest specifically Christian hymn in existence. The hymn illustrates perfectly the first part of the verse. Before they were baptized, they were submerged in the darkness of death; on being baptized, they arose from the dead into the light of Christ. In other words, what was dark became light. This association of light with baptism was so strong in the early church that the verb **phôtizô**, 'I shine upon', became a synonym for 'I baptize'.

15 So watch carefully how you live – not as foolish people [do] but as sensible ones, 16 not squandering your time since the days are evil. 17 For this reason, do not be stupid, but understand what the will of the Lord

[is]. 18 And do not get drunk on wine, a form of profligacy, but be filled with the Spirit, 19 communicating with each other with psalms, hymns and spiritual songs, singing and playing music to the Lord with your heart, 20 expressing your thanks at all times for everything in the name of our Lord Jesus Christ to God our Father,

[15] 'Carefully', **akrîbôs**, is placed by some manuscripts after 'how', hence the AV has 'that ye walk circumspectly', but **akrîbôs** is commonly used with verbs of knowing and perceiving, not with verbs denoting behaviour. In other words, it is not usually a moral term. The adjective **akrîbês**, however, can mean 'precise', 'strict', 'puritanical' or 'stingy'. Nevertheless, the best manuscripts compel us to take **akrîbôs** with 'watch'.

[16] 'Squandering the time'; see the notes on Col. 4.5.

[17] 'Stupid', **aphrones**, i.e. 'senseless' or 'brainless'.

[18] 'A form of profligacy', **en hôi estin asôtiâ**, literally, 'in which is wastefulness'. **Asôtiâ** is the vice of the spendthrift or the profligate, who squanders his money on riotous living. 'In which' refers to the activity of drinking to excess, not to the adjacent noun 'wine'.

[19] For this and the next verse refer to the parallel passage Col. 3.16–17.

'Communicating', literally, 'saying', **lalountes**. It may seem odd to use the verb 'say' to denote singing, but Pliny (Book 10, letter 96) describes the Christians, whom he had interrogated about their practices, as admitting that they 'say', *dicere*, a hymn to Christ.

'Playing music', **psallontes**, literally, 'plucking'. It would appear that the music was played on stringed instruments. It does not follow, however, that all their singing was accompanied.

'*With* your heart' (singular, despite the plural form of the pronoun 'your'), not '*in* your heart'. This does not mean 'to yourself', i.e. 'privately', but 'heartily', 'with feeling' or, as Chrysostom says, 'applying yourselves [to it] with understanding'. The message of vv. 18 and 19 is that the Christian should avoid drunken parties where people sing doubtful songs, and instead join fellow Christians at celebrations of a spiritual nature where a different kind of song is sung.

[20] 'For everything', **hyper pantôn**, not 'for (on behalf of) everyone'.

21 giving way to one another in the fear of Christ, 22 wives to their husbands, as though to the Lord, 23 because a husband is the head of his wife as Christ is also the head of his church, being himself the saviour of his body. 24 But as the church is subject to Christ, so wives, too, [are subject] to their husbands in every respect.

[21–24] It might be useful to start by stating what Paul is *not* saying in this passage: firstly, he does not say that women are subject to men; in fact, he adds the emphatic **idiois** 'to their own' to make it clear that the noun it describes, **andrasin**, refers here to 'husbands' and not 'men', its common meaning. Hence, he is talking about 'wives', not 'women'. Secondly, he does not say that only women, or wives, are to 'give way', 'submit themselves'; *all* Christians have just been described as 'giving way' to one another. Thirdly, 'giving way', 'submitting themselves', **hypotassomenoi**, is a voluntary act, not the compulsory action of a slave; nor is it blind obedience.

To understand this passage, which is much more complex than the parallel passage Col. 3.18, we should bear in mind that Paul is working out an allegory; the relation of husband to wife on earth is seen as an illustration of his great theme, i.e. Christ as the head of his body. As he points out in v.32, his subject is not marriage but the relationship between Christ and his church. In I Cor. 11.3 the statement that the husband is the head of the wife, as Christ is the head of the husband, and God the head of Christ, foreshadows the more developed doctrine we find here. There are significant differences. For instance, in the Corinthians passage Christ is not called the head of the church, and in the Ephesians version, the headship of God over Christ is not mentioned.

[22] Note that there is no verb in this verse. Some manuscripts add either 'let them give way' or '(you) give way', but it is unnecessary to add a verb.

[23] The headship of Christ is bound up with his function as saviour. Hence the husband's headship over his wife necessarily involves some self-sacrifice. This is spelled out in v. 25. It should also be noted that being the head of the body does not mean that the head can dispense with the services of the other parts of the body. As Paul points out in I Cor. 12.21, the head cannot say to the feet, 'I don't need you'. The notion of headship should not be considered in abstract; it is the head of a living body that we are talking about, a body where all the parts are necessary for the proper functioning of the whole.

[24] 'Is subject', or 'submits itself', **hypotassetai**. The AV and the NEB assume that the verb governed by 'wives', which is omitted in the Greek, is a command, and add 'let [them] be [subject]', and 'must be [subject]', respectively. The Vulgate, like the Greek, omits the verb. It is better to treat the missing verb as a statement of fact, since Paul is demonstrating the *fact* that the church is subject to Christ from the *fact* that wives are subject to their husbands. At this point of the argument, Paul is not telling wives that they *ought* to be subject to their

husbands, but pointing out to them that their actual married state is like that of the church in relation to Christ.

25 Husbands, love your wives, as Christ loved his church and gave himself for her, 26 in order to sanctify her, having purified her by the washing with water [and] by the word, 27 in order that he might personally present the church to himself, glorious, without spot or blemish or any such thing, so that she might be holy and blameless.

[25] The image of the church as the bride of Christ is echoed in Isa. 62.5 (AV), 'as the bridegroom rejoiceth over the bride, so shall thy God rejoice over thee'.

Having established that marriage is an imitation of the relationship between Christ and his church, Paul now exhorts husbands to follow Christ's example of love and self-sacrifice. This verse should be recalled whenever Paul's teaching is criticized on the grounds that he preaches the exploitation of women by men.

[26] There are three distinct ideas running through this and the next verse: the image of the newly baptized Christian, the image of the bride being prepared for her wedding, and the image of the suitable animal being selected for sacrifice.

Sanctification and baptism are also associated in I Cor. 6.11, 'But you have been washed, you have been sanctified, you have been justified in the name of the Lord Jesus Christ and in the Spirit of our God.'

'[And] by the word', **en rhêmati**, literally, 'in the word'. This must refer to the formula accompanying the act of baptism, although some commentators try to prove that it refers to the gospel or some scriptural teaching. It has even been suggested that 'by the word' should be taken with 'sanctify'. Early commentators, however, saw that the 'word' was the formula used during the ritual of baptism. Augustine observed (*Tracts on John*, 80), 'Take away the word, and what is water but mere water? The word is added to the element and it becomes a sacrament (*accedit verbum ad elementum et fit sacramentum*).' Chrysostom asks 'What word?', and answers the question himself, 'in the name of the Father and of the Son and of the Holy Spirit'. For the difference between **rhêma** and **logos**, see my notes on 1.3 and 6.5 in *Reading Through Hebrews*.

[27] 'Personally (i.e. himself) present', **parastêsêi autos**, because the bride is normally presented to the bridegroom by somebody else. The metaphor of the bride is also found in II Cor. 11.2, where Paul depicts himself as the marriage broker, or the best man, presenting the Corinthians as a collective bride to Christ, 'I have betrothed you to one husband, *to present* you (**parastêsai**) as a holy virgin to Christ.'

'Without spot or blemish', **mê echousan spilon ê rhytida**, would seem to refer to the physical appearance of the beautiful bride, but **spilos** can also have a moral sense. In II Peter 2.13, the only other place where it occurs in the NT, it is used metaphorically of the wicked brethren, '*spots* (**spiloi**) and *blemishes* (**mômoi**), luxuriating in their deceits as they feast together with you'. **Rhytis** is not found anywhere else in the NT. Its usual meaning in classical literature is 'wrinkle'.

'Holy and blameless', **hagiâ kai amômos**, as I point out in the notes on Col. 1.22, is a description associated with the sacrifices of the Mosaic Law.

28 This is how husbands, too, should love their own wives, as their own bodies. He who loves his own wife loves himself. 29 For no one ever hated his own flesh, but [everyone] nourishes and cherishes it, just as Christ [does] the church, 30 because we are members of his body. 31 'For this reason a man shall leave his father and mother and be joined to his wife; and the two shall

be one flesh.' 32 This secret truth is a great thing (I am speaking about Christ and his church). 33 But you also, let each one of you individually love his wife as himself, and a wife should respect her husband.

[28] This vision of the wife as being part of her husband's body is subtle; she is his flesh, and he is hers. They are, in a profound sense, each other. Furthermore, the word 'love', **agapân**, one hardly needs to point out, is not 'fall in love' or 'be passionately drawn towards', but is the manifestation of commitment characterized by self-sacrifice and continuing care. Note also that there is nothing wrong in 'loving' oneself. It is not narcissism (that would be the meaning of 'love' which I have just rejected) to care for and look after oneself.

'As their own bodies' does not mean '*as they do* their own bodies' but '*as being* their own bodies', in other words, 'since their wives are their own bodies'.

[29] 'Cherishes', **thalpei**, is a very warm word in Greek. Paul uses it in I Thess. 2.7, where he compares himself to a nursing mother '*cuddling* (**thalpêi**) her own children'.

[30] 'Of his body' is followed in some manuscripts by 'from his flesh, and from his bones', probably because it was suggested by Gen. 2.23 (Sept.), 'And Adam said, "This is now bone from my bones, and flesh from my flesh".'

[31] This is from Gen. 2.24. The original had **heneken** instead of **anti**, 'for', but otherwise the quotation is very close to the Sept. version from which it has been taken.

The key statement here is 'the two shall be one flesh', which Paul now applies to the relationship between Christ and his bride, but early commentators saw an additional allegory in this verse. For instance, Jerome says, 'The first prophet Adam prophesied this regarding Christ and the church, because our

Lord and Saviour left his father, God, and his mother, the heavenly Jerusalem.'

[32] 'Secret truth', **mystêrion,** is virtually the equivalent of the Hebrew word *hiddush,* a term used by rabbis when revealing some hidden truth in scripture which no one has spotted before. See also the note on Col. 1.26. The OT passage is discovered to have another meaning, a truth which has now been revealed in Christ, i.e. that the marriage relationship is an allegory of the relationship between Christ and his church. As Hodge points out, 'It is the union between Christ and his people, the fact that they are one flesh, that he declares to be a great mystery.'

[33] The sudden shift in thought, the ungrammatical leap from 'you' (second person plural) to the third person plural **hoi kath'hena,** 'individually', then to the third person singular **hekastos agapâtô,** 'let each one love', together with the juxtaposition of the imperative **agapâtô** with the subjunctive **phobêtai,** are all typical of Paul's style. He leaves his main theme of the mystery of Christ's marriage to his bride the church, but not without reminding husbands to love their wives, and wives to respect, literally, 'fear', hence 'revere', **phobêtai,** their husbands. This introduces a final passage of moral exhortation and homily.

# Chapter 6

1 Children, obey your parents in the Lord; for this is right. 2 'Honour your father and mother'; this is the first commandment with a promise, 3 'that it may go well for you and that you may live long on the earth'. 4 And you fathers, do not make your children angry, but bring them up with the discipline and instruction of the Lord.

[1] 'In the Lord' is an awkward phrase and is missing in some manuscripts. Perhaps it crept into the text from the parallel passage in Colossians (3.20). Is the writer saying that children should obey their Christian parents (not their pagan ones)? Are the children described as being 'in the Lord', or their parents, or both? It is probable that the phrase means something like 'following the commandments of Christ', or 'conforming to Christian teaching'.

[2] The commandment quoted is from Ex. 20.12 or Deut. 5.16.

'With a promise', **en epangeliâi,** refers to the promise quoted in the next verse. It is described as the 'first with a promise' because it is the first in the list of the ten commandments, indeed it is the only one, with a positive promise of a benefit accruing to those who keep the commandment. Some commandments speak of the punishment which will fall upon defaulters.

[3] There is a slight variation from the Sept. version, i.e **esêi makrochronios**, instead of **hina makrochronios genêi**. This is typical of quotations from memory.


[4] This verse, at first impression, seems to imply that fathers have a choice: either to make their children angry, or to educate them. This is not the intended meaning. Paul is saying, 'When you discipline and educate your children, don't make them resentful by your heavy-handed treatment of them.' The Colossians version (3.21) warns fathers to avoid causing their children to lose heart.

'Discipline', **paideiâi**, literally, 'child-rearing'. This is the normal Greek word for 'education'.

'Instruction of the Lord', in other words, Christian or religious education.


5 Slaves, obey your earthly masters with fear and trembling in the simplicity of your heart as though [they were] Christ, 6 not in a show of service like those who aim to please human beings, but like slaves of Christ, doing the will of God from your soul, 7 serving them with good will as though [they were] the Lord and not human beings, 8 knowing that each one of you, if he does any good deed, will receive it back from the Lord, whether he is a slave or a freeman. 9 And you masters, do the same to them, give up threats, knowing that the Master both of them and of you is in heaven and there is no partiality with him.


[5–8] This section is very similar to Col. 3.22–25. It is impossible to demonstrate that either one must be an imitation of the other. The simpler hypothesis is that both passages are written by the same person. Since much of the vocabulary and many of the phrases occur in Colossians, the relevant notes will also apply here.

[5] 'With fear and trembling' is a typical Pauline phrase found also in I Cor. 2.3; II Cor. 7.15 and Phil. 2.12. No other NT author uses it.

[6] 'Slaves' can also be translated as 'servants'.

[7] As I point out in the note to Col. 3.24, 'Lord', **Kûrios**, also means 'Master'. The earthly 'masters' are to be treated as though they were the heavenly 'Master'.

[8] Col. 3.25 speaks of being punished for the wrong one does, not of being rewarded for good deeds.

[9] 'The Master . . . is in heaven' rather than 'there is a Master in heaven', since there is a definite article attached to 'Master'. Col. 4.1 does not have the definite article with 'Master'. Paul is making the point that it is in *heaven*, not on earth, that there is no distinction between slave and free. This point is not spelled out in the Col. 4.1 parallel version, since the reference to partiality occurs in an earlier verse.

10 From now on, be empowered by the Lord and by the might of his strength. 11 Put on the full armour of God so that you can stand against the crafty tricks of the devil, 12 because our struggle is not against flesh and blood but against the rulers and authorities, against the world-masters of this darkness, against the spirit powers of wickedness in the heavenly places.

[10] 'From now on', **tou loipou**. Some manuscripts have the commoner expression **to loipon**, but there is little difference in meaning betwen them, and **tou loipou** occurs also in Gal. 6.17. 'Hereafter' or 'finally' are also possible meanings.

'Be empowered', **endynamousthe,** i.e. 'take the power of', not 'be strong' (AV), which nowadays tends to mean the same as 'be brave'.

'Might of his strength' occurs also in 1.19. See the notes on that verse.

[11] 'Crafty tricks', **methodeiâs,** a word which is also used in 4.14 but nowhere else in the NT, although it is found in the Septuagint. Originally it meant 'method of procedure', 'way of doing something', hence, 'stratagem', and so 'trickery'.

[12] 'Rulers and authorities' are either the angelic powers, as in 3.10, or some other spiritual forces. This time they are definitely evil or demonic. In the earlier passage they are not necessarily evil.

'World-masters', **kosmokratoras,** was a term often used by the rabbis to refer to powerful kings such as Nebuchadnezzar or Belshazzar, and also to spiritual powers such as the Angel of Death. II Cor.4.4 speaks of Satan as 'the god of this age' and John 12.31 refers to 'the ruler of this world', **ho archôn tou kosmou toutou.** 'The power of darkness' of Col. 1.13 is probably Satan. As our passage speaks of the 'world-masters of this *darkness*', the Corinthians passage seems particularly appropriate because it goes on to say, 'he blinded the minds of the faithless so that the *light* of the glorious gospel of Christ should not shine upon them'. The problem, however, is that the 'world-masters' are plural and so most probably refer to the pagan deities Paul's audience used to worship. **Kosmokratores** is used in astrology to refer to the sun and the moon, together with the planets. We also find reference to the 'seven' **kosmokratores,** in other words the deities associated with the days of the week, Apollo, Artemis, Ares, Hermes, etc.

'The spirit powers', **ta pneumatika,** are not another group of powers but most probably the 'world-masters' already mentioned.

'In the heavenly places' is not a reference to the spiritual heaven where God is, as it is in 1.3; 1.20 and 2.6, but the regions where the planetary powers are thought to be situated. See the notes on 1.3 regarding this phrase. There were, of course, seven heavens with their appropriate inhabitants. Paul refers in II Cor. 12.2 to the third heaven.

13 For this reason, take up the full armour of God, so that you can withstand on the evil day, and when you have done everything, stand. 14 So stand with your loins girded by truth and wearing the breastplate of righteousness, 15 with your feet shod with the readiness of the gospel of peace. 16 In all things, take up the shield of faith, with which you will be able to quench all the flaming missiles of the evil one, 17 and receive the helmet of salvation and the sword of the Spirit, which is the word of God.

[13] 'Withstand', **antistênai**, and 'stand', **stênai**, are a deliberate play on words. Col. 4.12 clearly uses 'stand' in the context of standing before the judgment seat of God. Here we seem to have a double meaning, standing firm in battle, and standing triumphant before God's judgment seat.

'The evil day' is either the day of judgment or a time of temptation or trial.

'When you have done everything', in other words, 'when you have done all that you can do', rather than 'when you have overcome all opposition'.

[14] 'Loins girded by truth', **perizôsamenoi tên osphyn en alêtheiâi,** is a conflation of Isa. 11.5 (Sept.), 'And his *loins* (**osphyn**) will be *girded* (**ezôsmenos**) by righteousness, and his sides covered by *truth* (**alêtheiâi**).'

'Wearing the breastplate of righteousness', **endûsamenoi ton thôrâka tês dikaiosynês,** comes from Isa. 59.17 (Sept.), 'he put on righteousness as a breastplate', **enedûsato dikaiosynên hôs thôrâka.** The metaphor is also found in Wisdom 5.18.

[15] 'Readiness', **hetoimasiâi**, rather than 'preparation', be-cause it denotes readiness to go out and spread the gospel, not the state of being well-prepared. The reference to 'feet' shows that movement is necessary here. The adjective 'ready', **het-oimos**, can also mean 'willing', 'zealous' or 'active'. The paradox of the Christian warrior armed with the gospel of peace is deliberate. As Chrysostom observes, 'If we fight with the devil, we are at peace with God.'

[16] 'In all things', **en pâsin**, i.e. 'in all situations' or 'at all times'. The AV has 'above all' because it is based on a text which read **epi pâsin**, 'in addition to all [things]'.

'Shield', together with the 'helmet' and the 'sword' of the next verse, would seem to be an echo of Wisdom 5.18–20, 'and he will put on as a *helmet* unfeigned judgment; he will take holiness as an unconquerable *shield* and sharpen his relentless anger as a *sword*'.

[17] 'Helmet of salvation' is an abbreviated form of Paul's earlier phrase in I Thess. 5.8, 'as a helmet, the hope of salvation'.

'Which' here is neuter, **ho**, not the feminine **hê**, the normal relative used when referring to a feminine noun such as 'sword', **machairan**. Hence some commentators argue that 'which' refers to the neuter 'Spirit'. There are, however, several examples of Paul using the neuter relative pronoun when referring to masculine or feminine nouns: Col. 3.14 and II Thess. 3.17, for instance. It is also just as likely that he is referring loosely to the whole phrase 'sword of the Spirit', rather than to a single noun.

'Word', **rhêma**, here stands for the scriptures, which one might expect to be described as **logos**. There is a reason for this; the emphasis here is on the scriptures as a creative principle, 'the sword of the Spirit', i.e. the word in action. See the notes on 5.26.

18 Pray at every opportunity in the Spirit with every kind of prayer and supplication, keeping watch for this purpose with all perseverance and supplication for all the saints, 19 and also for me, that I may be given the words when I open my mouth to make known with boldness the secret of the gospel, 20 for the sake of which I am an ambassador in chains, that I may by the same speak freely in the way that I should.

[18] 'Supplication', **deêseôs**, i.e. 'entreaty'. Note the awkward repetition of this word.

'Keeping watch', **agrypnountes**, literally, 'staying awake', a synonym for **grêgorountes** in the Col. 4.2 version.

[19] This must refer to Paul's impending court appearance before the authorities.

'With boldness', **en parrhêsiâi**, literally, 'in free speech', occurs also in Col.2.15. See the notes on that verse.

'Secret', **mystêrion**; see note on Col. 1.26. This is the sixth appearance of the word in this letter. It is interesting that the Vulgate translates **mystêrion** by *sacramentum* four times and twice leaves it as *mysterium*. There seems to be no reason for this variation, unless it indicates that the translator felt that word had no real equivalent in Latin.

[20] 'For the sake of which I am an ambassador in chains' is a splendid paradox, since official ambassadors are never chained. It is more poetical than the Colossians phrase 'because of which I am in prison'.

'That I may speak freely', **hina parrhêsiasômai**, is best taken as another clause governed by 'pray' in v. 18, rather than as a purpose clause, i.e. 'in order that I may speak freely'.

'By the same', **en autôi**, is a difficult phrase. One or two manuscripts have instead **auto**, 'it', which would refer to the 'secret' or the 'gospel'. Although the variation in reading is dubious, it could point to the fact that the better reading **en autôi** also refers to the 'secret' or the 'gospel'. If so, we should perhaps translate **en** as 'about' or 'in respect of'. If, on the other hand, it refers to the 'word[s]', **logos**, as seems more likely, the instrumental 'by' or 'with' would make sense. 'The same' cannot refer to 'chains' because the genders do not agree. Some might like to translate **en autôi** as 'in him', i.e. Christ, but, as he has not been mentioned for some time, such a reference is impossible.

21 Tychicus, my beloved brother and faithful servant in the Lord, will give you all the information, so that you, too, may know about my situation and how I am doing. 22 I have sent him to you for this very purpose, so that you may know about our situation and so that he can boost your morale. 23 Peace to the brethren and love with faith from God the Father and the Lord Jesus Christ. 24 Grace be with all who love our Lord Jesus Christ in eternity.

[21] 'Tychicus': see note on Col. 4.7.

[22] This verse is the same as Col. 4.8. It is clearly a standard formula, and no doubt occurred in other letters of Paul which have not survived.

[23] 'Love with faith', **agapê meta pisteôs**, i.e. 'love accompanied by faith'.

[24] 'In eternity', **en aphtharsiâi**, Vulg. *in incorruptione*. **Aphtharsiâ** is 'incorruptibility', hence 'immortality', a word used only by Paul in the NT and familiar to us from the famous passage on the resurrection towards the end of I Cor. 15. The adjective **aphthartos**, 'incorruptible' or 'immortal',

also meant 'unfading', 'eternal'. The AV's 'in sincerity' can only go with 'those that love', whereas 'in eternity' can also go with 'grace'.

# Bibliography

T. K. Abbott, *Epistles to the Ephesians and to the Colossians: A Critical and Exegetical Commentary*, The International Critical Commentary, T. & T. Clark, Edinburgh 1897 (reprinted 1964)

F. F. Bruce, *Commentary on the Epistle to the Colossians*, The New International Commentary on the New Testament, W. B. Eerdmans, Grand Rapids, Michigan 1957

C. Gore, *St Paul's Epistle to the Ephesians*, John Murray, London 1905

C. Hodge, *Ephesians*, Crossway Books, Illinois 1994 (originally published as *A Commentary on the Epistle to the Ephesians*, Banner of Truth Trust, London 1964)

J. B. Lightfoot, *St Paul's Epistles to the Colossians and to Philemon*, Macmillan & Co., London 1879

*Notes on Epistles of St Paul from unpublished commentaries*, Macmillan and Co., London 1895

Ralph P. Martin, *Colossians: The Church's Lord and the Christian's Liberty*, Paternoster Press, Exeter 1972

C. F. D. Moule, *The Epistles of Paul the Apostle to the Colossians and to Philemon*, The Cambridge Greek Testament Commentary, Cambridge University Press, Cambridge 1957

Dan Cohn-Sherbok, *The Jewish Faith*, SPCK, London 1993

E. K. Simpson, *Commentary on the Epistle to the Ephesians*, The New International Commentary on the New Testament, W. B. Eerdmans, Grand Rapids, Michigan 1957

F. C. Synge, *Philippians and Colossians*, Torch Bible Commentaries, SCM Press, London 1951

G. H. P. Thompson, *The Letters of Paul to the Ephesians, to the Colossians and to Philemon*, The Cambridge Bible Commentary on the New English Bible, Cambridge University Press, Cambridge 1967